The Lorenzaccio Story

First published 1978 by Pluto Press Limited
Unit 10 Spencer Court, 7 Chalcot Road, London NW1 8LH

The music, by Stephen Oliver, is obtainable
in manuscript from London Management,
235–241 Regent Street, London W1A 2JT

ISBN 0 904383 85 7

Designed by Tom Sullivan
Cover designed by David King
Cover picture: Agnolo Bronzino, *Venus, Cupid, Folly and Time*,
1545. Reproduced by Courtesy of the Trustees, The National Gallery,
London.

Printed in Great Britain by Latimer Trend & Company Ltd Plymouth

Paul Thompson
after Alfred de Musset

The Lorenzaccio Story

Scenario devised
in collaboration with
Ron Daniels

Music by
Stephen Oliver

Pluto  Plays

The Lorenzaccio Story

At the beginning of the sixteenth century the citizens of Florence witnessed the capitalist spirit of risk and danger degenerating into self-indulgence. They sought safe investment in land, they looked for security, they devoted themselves to luxury and in a climate of self-betrayal they began to forsake the old 'economic' way of life on which their existence depended.

Having lost the initiative to their trading rivals the Florentine economy went into decline. Frequent changes of government failed to stop the rot and finally the Florentines suffered the humiliation of military defeat and occupation by the imperial forces of Charles V.

In 1531 Charles V appointed, as Duke of Florence, the twenty-year-old Alessandro who has been described by historians as a corrupt and hedonistic tyrant who maintained power by force. Alessandro governed Florence for six years until the night of 5 January 1537 when he was assassinated by his most trusted friend Lorenzo.

The events of 1537 provided the background for Alfred de Musset's play *Lorenzaccio*. The play was written in 1833 and its literary derivation can be traced to Varchi's *History of Florence*, Schiller's *Conspiracy of Fiezo in Genoa* and George Sand's *Conspiracy in 1537*.

Ron Daniels and I were attracted to *Lorenzaccio* for a number of reasons, not least of which is the fact that de Musset provides a marvellous story set within a fascinating period of history. Although we were attracted by the de Musset play, at the same time we felt challenged by it. In the character of Lorenzo, de Musset had created the archetypal bourgeois hero, romantic, individualistic and self-obsessed. He also offered a view of history which glorified the individual and denigrated the mass.

The Lorenzaccio Story is a provocative response to de Musset's provocative vision.

During the research for the play I had access to material that would not have been available to de Musset, but my play is no more historically accurate than the original. I have simply retold the de Musset play from a different political perspective, showing how this act of tyrannicide failed to precipitate an uprising and remained the isolated action of one individual, the motivation for which is questionable.

In the process of retelling the story I have eliminated some characters and introduced others. Many are given long monologues where they justify to the audience their actions or excuse their failure to act. I have emphasised the class structure of Florentine society and have invited the audience to see the story of Lorenzo and Alessandro through the eyes of the 'poor man', the man who is about to assassinate the assassin. The poor man has never visited the the weird and wonderful world of Florence, he can only imagine what life would have been like there. It is he who begins and ends the play; he should also be used wherever possible in all the servile roles throughout the action simply to remind an audience of his presence.

Another major departure from de Musset is the introduction of songs which are used to strengthen this new perspective. The music is by Stephen Oliver who has employed references to and echoes from a variety of periods and styles. The same principle was applied to the designs by Chris Dyer and Jenny Beavan, where khaki jackets and PVC cloaks were mingled with Renaissance costume.

Ron Daniels's production for the Royal Shakespeare Company was staged in the round. The acting area was simply an open space containing junk, clothes, boxes, a few broken-down chairs, a table or two and any props necessary for the production. The action unfolded as if it were a tale re-enacted by ghosts on the proverbial scrapheap of history.

Each setting was suggested in the simplest manner possible, the mere placing of a chair defined an interior or exterior location and the action flowed freely without interruption for scene changes.

Paul Thompson

The Lorenzaccio Story was first produced on 21 July 1977 at The Other Place, the Royal Shakespeare Company's studio theatre at Stratford-upon-Avon. The cast was as follows:

A Man	Ian McNeice
Lorenzo	Peter McEnery
Duke Alessandro de' Medici	James Laurenson
Filippo Strozzi	David Swift
Piero Strozzi	Simon Rouse
Cardinal Cibo	Morris Perry
Captain Vitelli	John Rhys-Davies
Laudomia	Charlotte Cornwell
A Goldsmith	John Burgess
Tebaldeo	Ian Gelder
Francesco Vettori	Desmond Stokes
Luisa	Roberta Taylor
Bindo	Desmond Stokes
Bellini	Alan David
Scoronconcolo	Ian McNeice
Francesco Alamanni	Dominic Jephcott
Cosimo de' Medici	James Laurenson
A Girl	Roberta Taylor
A Stonemason	Ian McNeice
A Servant (employed by Filippo Strozzi)	Ian McNeice
A Servant (employed by Francesco Vettori)	Ian McNeice
Emperor Charles the Fifth	Dominic Jephcott

Members of the company also played Exiles,
Prisoners, Monks, Soldiers and Cardinals
Directed by Ron Daniels
Music by Stephen Oliver
Designed by Chris Dyer and Jenny Beavan
After the season at Stratford-upon-Avon the part of Tebaldeo was played by Peter Clough and the part of Filippo Strozzi by Graham Crowden.

PROLOGUE

An open space. Enter LORENZO. *After a few moments a* MAN *enters. He is obviously poor.*

Lorenzo You've been following me. Why?

Man I need the money.

Lorenzo Are you frightened?

Man Yes.

Lorenzo Shall we talk first?

Man I've got nothing to say.

Lorenzo Will you listen to me?

Man It won't make any difference.

ACT 1

SCENE 1

LORENZO *and the* MAN *remain on stage.* DUKE ALESSANDRO's *voice is heard off-stage.*

Duke (*voice off*) Lorenzo? (*pause*) Lorenzo?

LORENZO *sits, he takes out a prayer book and begins to read.*

Lorenzo (*reading*) Deign to look with compassion, Lord, upon these offerings I lay before thee: the struggles of the poor, the perils of nations, the groans of captives, the desolation of orphans, the hardships of travellers, the helplessness of cripples, the anguish of the incurably sick, the failing strength of the aged, young men's sighs, the yearning of maidens, the grief of widows.

Duke ALESSANDRO *enters.*

(*continues reading*) For thou, Lord, art full of pity for all mankind, and hatest nothing which thou hast made.

Duke One of us is dreaming.

Lorenzo (*offering the* DUKE *the prayer book*) A gift from Lorenzo to the Duke of Florence.

Duke Or drunk.

Lorenzo Don't you like my present?

Duke A prayer book?

Lorenzo Of course. (*to* MAN) At that moment I sent my servant to fetch the costumes.

The MAN *goes.*

Duke Lorenzo, you made a promise to me.

Lorenzo Have I ever disappointed you? Undress.

Duke Now?

Lorenzo Do you trust me?

LORENZO *takes off his shirt.*

Duke (*smiles*) With my life.

DUKE *undresses apart from his vest of chain mail.*

Lorenzo Yet you keep your chain mail on?

The DUKE *laughs. The* MAN *returns with two nuns' habits.*

Duke Is that what I think it is?

Lorenzo The key to the gates of paradise.

The DUKE *holds up a costume.*

Duke Your choice flatters me, Lorenzo.
Lorenzo My Lord, we are dead to the fashions of this world.
Duke Right.

They help each other dress.

Lorenzo Eternal Father, give me back the robes of innocence which I received
in baptism . . . and keep it undefiled upon me, lest I be shut out from
paradise.
Duke Do we need money?
Lorenzo Christ Jesus clothe me in the garb of thine own fragrant virtues . . .
of humility, patience, charity and chastity . . . so that I may obtain thy
heavenly Father's blessing.
Duke Look after my purse, Lorenzo.
Lorenzo Holy Spirit, adorn me with the many coloured coat of thy gifts . . .
so that I may find favour in thy sight.
Lorenzo/Duke Amen.
Lorenzo With this ring I thee wed.
Duke With this ring I thee wed.
Lorenzo We are now the brides of Christ.
Duke Of all the angels, Lorenzo, you are the sweetest.
Lorenzo Your prayer book, my lord.

CARNIVAL SONG

The song should begin as LORENZO *and the* DUKE *are dressing. The actors
take individual lines as they make their individual entrances, interrupting
the dialogue.*

> Are you ready?
>> Have you got your wig on straight?
> Where's my lipstick?
>> Do these stockings suit my costume?
> Are you happy?
> Where's my mask?
> Is that a new dress?
> Come on let's go.
> You're looking perfect.
> Have a good time.
> You're looking perfect.
> Have a good time.

*The whole cast is on stage, they are dressed and made up for a carnival.
The* MAN *watches in amazement.*

All   Have a good time while you can 'cos life is short.
Have some fun while you're young and you've got money.
What does it matter if you're living on a cliff-edge.
    Enjoy the view
    The danger too
    Can be exciting.

Have a good time while you can 'cos life is short
Take out a friend, show him all that he's been missing
What does it matter if the world is so depressing
    Have some wine
    It's not a crime
    Your glass is empty.

Have a good time, can't you hear the band is playing
A final fling, one more time and then another
What does it matter if you're dancing on a tightrope.
    Enjoy the thrill of being young
    Death dances off with everyone
    Death dances off with everyone.

The actors now take individual lines as they make individual exits.

Are you ready?
    Have you got your wig on straight?
Where's my lipstick?
    Do these stockings suit my costume?
Are you happy?
Where's my mask?
Is that a new dress?
Come on, let's go.
You're looking perfect.
Have a good time.
You're looking perfect.
Have a good time.

The GOLDSMITH *and the* SILK MERCHANT *remain on stage.*

SCENE 2

A street. Early morning. The GOLDSMITH *and the* SILK MERCHANT *are opening their shops. Music continues under this scene.*

Merchant Beautiful morning.

Goldsmith Diabolical night. Listen to it. Still going on. They turn night into day, day into night, they never meet any normal people.

Merchant They're not normal people, are they. They're the nobility.

Goldsmith HUH!

The GOLDSMITH *begins to construct an elaborate display.*

Merchant Do you know what I did last night?

Goldsmith Enlighten me.

Merchant Laid back in bed. Opened the windows and enjoyed it. I fell asleep to the sound of violins. I tried to imagine all those lords and ladies having a good time. The entire aristrocracy of Florence dressed up in my beautiful silks.

Goldsmith Did you manage to see the ones they hadn't paid for? They're the ones they spilled wine down, trailed in the dirt and rubbed against the wall. It's all right for them. They lead a great life. Horse-back riding, hunting, dancing. One continual round of pleasure. Drinking, gambling, debauchery, disgusting.

Merchant It's different for them. They're born to it.

Goldsmith And we pay for it.

Merchant Well, at least they brighten the place up. They add a little colour. Pageantry.

Goldsmith I could do without colour in my life thank you. Look at these.

(GOLDSMITH *indicates damaged goblets*) That was yesterday. The Carnival. When they dragged the balloon up the street.

Merchant Who did it?

Goldsmith The Strozzi family.

Merchant They'll pay.

Goldsmith Will they?

Merchant Oh yes, very decent people the Strozzi.

Goldsmith How do you know?

Merchant My wife said so.

Goldsmith Let me tell you something. There is no such thing as a decent person in Florence. They're all out for what they can get. This city, my friend, is finished. Even the banks are closing down. No confidence. I tell you, the moment I find someone fool enough to buy me out, I'm off.

The GOLDSMITH *finishes his display.*

What do you think of that?

Merchant Very clever.

Goldsmith That is a display, that is. Eye-catching. That'll bring 'em in.

Merchant What if someone knocks it over again?

Goldsmith Listen. If you want to make money in business. You've got to learn to take risks.

PIERO *and* TEBALDEO *enter.* TEBALDEO *picks up a goblet.*

Careful with that sir.

Tebaldeo It's beautiful.

Goldsmith Five florins.

Tebaldeo Can't afford it. I'm an artist.

Goldsmith Let's put it back then, eh?

Piero I'm Piero Strozzi.
Goldsmith My lord. (*He bows*)
Piero I've come about the damage to your goods.
Goldsmith Damage? Oh, yes. Sixteen florins.

PIERO *pays.*

I don't like to accept the money. But, you know how it is. I have to pay
my apprentices whether I sell anything or not.
Piero I see the ball's still going on.
Goldsmith You didn't attend yourselves?
Piero We don't like the company.
Goldsmith Nice music.
Merchant (*to* PIERO) How are you enjoying yourself at university?
Piero Fine.
Merchant All the trouble they've had there. I expect you're a good influence.
Set 'em a good example.
Piero Listen, students don't enjoy living under this government. No more
than you enjoy paying for it with your taxes.
Merchant I try not to complain . . . but him! (*Indicates* GOLDSMITH.)

The MERCHANT *retires to his goods.*

Piero (*to* GOLDSMITH) Think about it, there's a fortress under construction.
Tebaldeo (*to* GOLDSMITH) What's it for?
Piero Soldiers in the streets. None of 'em fit to bear arms. Meanwhile, Duke
Alessandro can do what he wants. Ravish your daughters, drink your
wine, smash your windows . . .
Tebaldeo And you foot the bill.
Goldsmith (*to* MERCHANT) Hear that? Not much fun, is it?
LUISA *and* ALAMANNI *have entered, they are talking to the* SILK MERCHANT.
Alamanni Get me a pair of silk stockings.
Luisa For your wife?
Alamanni For you. If you let me put them on you.

Exit MERCHANT.

Piero Alamanni! You're talking to my sister.
Luisa Piero. Don't do anything stupid.
Alamanni Leave him. He likes being ridiculous.

ALAMANNI *embraces* LUISA. PIERO *separates them.*

Piero (*to* LUISA) Get home . . . You're behaving in public like a common whore.
Alamanni You amuse me Strozzi. Anyone would think that all the virtue in
Florence had taken refuge with your family.
Piero Collaborator!
Alamanni Coward! (*silence*) Coward.
Tebaldeo Let's go.

PIERO, LUISA and TEBALDEO *go.*

Goldsmith (*to* ALAMANNI) Now, calm down.
Alamanni Shut up!

ALAMANNI *grabs the* GOLDSMITH.

Goldsmith No. Not on my display.

Crash! Exit ALAMANNI.

Merchant (*re-enters*) What happened?
Goldsmith Nothing. It's just the end of my world. That's all. (*pause*) No. No.
Soon be Friday. We'll go to the fair at Monte Olivetti. We always do well
at the fair.
Merchant What are you going to sell?

The MERCHANT *and* GOLDSMITH *put away their goods.*

SONG

Goldsmith

I once had self-respect,
    and people called me Sir:
my wife looked up to me,
    and I looked down on her.
My children listened
    when I gave them advice.
Mistakes like that
    even kids don't make twice.

Merchant

Ah, how times change
from what they used to be,
when you and I, my friend,
had respectability.
We could afford
to live the life of lords:

Goldsmith

that was before
those cheap goods from abroad.

Merchant

Once I had respect
    in my employees' eyes.
Their loyalty was something
    money couldn't buy.

Is there a man
    could ask for anything more?
The rich stayed rich,
    and the poor stayed poor.

Merchant/Goldsmith

Ah, how times change, *etc.*

Merchant/Goldsmith

But now it's all too much
    for us to understand.
Commercial life's all overheads
    and underhand.
It's no use struggling
    to scrimp or to save:
to stay alive,
    you work yourself into the grave.

Merchant/Goldsmith

Ah, how times change
from what they used to be,
when you and I, my friend,
had respectability.
Now there's no way
a business can be run.
Something must happen,
something must be done.

They go.

SCENE 3

The Citadel. CAPTAIN VITELLI *alone.*

Vitelli (*to the audience*) There was a sickness, a disease, that swept through nations. It weakened the will, rotted the spirit. I'd seen it before and I saw it then. When the citizen regarded the soldier with contempt.

I was the Captain of the Duke's Guard. Ill-educated, ill-mannered, no ear for music, no eye for fashion, I was a soldier, and the art of war was what I knew. At home in the fortress, at home in the field, I had no need of family or of friends. I loved my duty, I loved my men. We understood each other.

Not for us to discuss the comparative merits of Scipio, Hannibal and Caesar. We never read the military classics, Onasander and Aelian had no relevance to our lives. And all the heroes of Sparta and Rome could teach us nothing. We were soldiers. We put our faith in gunpowder. The cannon, the arquebus, they sharpened the senses, they clarified the mind. The soldier understood gunpowder. He respected it.

But the Florentines were weak people. In love with art, in love with money. They were children. Dreaming of the glories of their past. They mocked our manners, made fun of our ignorance. They despised us. And we despised them.

In the name of the Emperor Charles the Fifth, it was my duty to defend Florence. And that was what I did. Prepared for external attack. Prepared for internal unrest. To the best of my ability I obeyed my orders. But we were badly paid, ill-equipped, defences in need of repair, citadel incomplete. I hoped that Duke Alessandro would appreciate that we needed money.

Enter DUKE ALESSANDRO *and the* STONEMASON.

Stonemason When will the bricks arrive your Highness?
Duke Don't worry. As soon as Cardinal Cibo raises the money.

Exit STONEMASON.

Vitelli But in the meantime, my lord, we're vulnerable.
Duke Flood the ditch.
Vitelli Eh?
Duke Divert the river. Flood the ditch.
Vitelli If you flood the ditch my lord, you flood the lower gunports.
Duke Well, that's the architect's fault.
Vitelli Yes, my lord.
Duke What are you afraid of Captain Vitelli? We've given them peace, we've given them work.
Vitelli It can't last.
Duke I know.

Enter CARDINAL CIBO.

Cibo My lord, I looked everywhere. I couldn't find you.
Duke Do we have a reply from the Court of Rome?
Cibo Yes, your Highness.
Duke Well?
Cibo We're waiting for you at the palace.
Duke Tell me here.

Pause.

Cibo His Holiness, Pope Paul III, sends a thousand benedictions to your Highness. His most ardent wish is for your prosperity.
Duke No money?
Cibo His Holiness fears that you have brought this crisis upon yourself. The people of Florence are not accustomed to absolute rule.
Duke Cardinal, I did not choose to be Duke of Florence, I was appointed by

Pope Clement, who was last heard of in hell. And as for the money-mad citizens of Florence, they've only got themselves to blame, their economy and their so-called democratic institutions collapsed through their own mis-management.

Cibo I am simply reporting a message I don't enjoy my task.

Duke What else did the Pope have to say?

Cibo The immorality of your court irritates His Holiness.

Duke What did you say?

Cibo The immorality of your court irritates the Pope. Your government will never command respect if you associate with Lorenzo de' Medici.

Duke The Pope is well informed Cardinal.

Cibo (*with charm*) Your reputation, my lord, is difficult to deny.

Vitelli With respect, your Highness, Lorenzo is a by-word for debauchery. People call him 'Lorenzaccio'.

Duke If debauchery upsets the Pope, how does he explain his bastard son? Immaculate conception?

Cibo The Pope is prepared to help. His terms are generous.

Duke I understand his terms Cardinal.

Cibo It's in your own interest, my lord.

Duke I like Lorenzo.

Cibo He's an atheist, he respects nothing. His friends are criminals, thieves, prostitutes. How can you believe anything he says?

Duke I like him.

Cibo Can you trust him?

Duke What do you mean?

Cibo Can you trust him?

Vitelli If you want my advice Lorenzo's dangerous.

Duke Are you afraid of him Captain Vitelli?

Vitelli I'm afraid of no-one.

Duke And you Cardinal, are you afraid of Lorenzo?

Cibo For myself? No. For you? Yes.

Duke Gentlemen, this is ridiculous, Lorenzo's a coward, afraid to carry a sword. He's a poet, a philosopher, he faints at the sight of blood. I don't expect you to understand. I enjoy his company. I love the man!

Cibo Can you afford him, my lord?

Duke Do you want to know the truth? (*pause*) I need him. He's absolutely indispensable to me. Everything I know about the republicans, I know through him. Everything I know about the exiles, I know through him. He has one undeniable genius – to make fools of my enemies. Filippo Strozzi treats him like a son! And Lorenzo reports back every meeting, every conversation. Yes, he's a dangerous man all right, but not to me.

Cibo Is that your reply?

LORENZO *has entered with* ALAMANNI.

Lorenzo My lord, I told you before, don't talk to strange men.

Duke (*to* CIBO) Look at him, Cardinal, a physical wreck. How could he frighten anyone?

Lorenzo Morning Vitelli. Nice piece of cloth.

Vitelli Sybarite.

Lorenzo You're wasted in the army.

Vitelli Sybarite!

Lorenzo Unfortunately Vitelli, a Sybarite is a resident of Sybaris. I'm a hedonist. Back to the dictionary.

Duke The Cardinal and Captain Vitelli have been talking about you, it seems they don't approve of our way of life.

Lorenzo Jealousy. I've no idea if that's a sin Cardinal, but if it is, I absolve you. No need to kiss my hand, I'm not a christian I have too much respect for human beings.

Cibo You have no respect for human beings, you treat them as objects for your lust.

Lorenzo I find you resistable Cardinal, Vitelli is another matter.

Vitelli What are you suggesting? I'm the Captain of the Duke's Guard.

Lorenzo I like soldiers Vitelli.

Vitelli Then behave like one!

VITELLI *draws his sword.*

Sorry.

VITELLI *sheaths his sword.*

Lorenzo If someone told you I was a swordsman, they were wrong. I don't own a sword. I'm a poet.

Duke Give Lorenzo a sword.

Lorenzo Why, my lord?

Duke You've been insulted, fight.

ALAMANNI *offers his sword.*

Duke Take the sword Lorenzo, I'll be your second.

LORENZO *doesn't move.*

Take it!

DUKE *forces* LORENZO *to take the sword.*

Lorenzo My lord, what have I done?

VITELLI *draws his sword again.*

Duke Fight!

Lorenzo I can't.

Duke I command you!

LORENZO *weakens.*

Vitelli Come on man! Face me!
Lorenzo Please my lord.

LORENZO *staggers*.

Duke Look, he's gone white. His legs are shaking. He's sick.
Vitelli Woman!

LORENZO *faints*.

Duke (*to* CIBO *and* VITELLI) Are you happy now? (*to* LORENZO) Come on Lorenzino, it's all over.

The DUKE *and* ALAMANNI *pick up* LORENZO.

Cibo Your Highness, we must complete the fortress. The Emperor insists.
Duke Did he insist on paying for it?
Cibo It is Captain Vitelli's duty to protect you, my lord.
Duke Well, Cardinal, since the Pope refuses to help, we have no alternative – the citizens of Florence.
Cibo If you increase taxation, there'll be a revolution.
Duke Borrow the money.
Cibo The last loan was at twelve per cent and they've still not been paid.
Duke For God's sake Cardinal, why should we appeal to their sense of commerce? What about their sense of patriotism? After all it's their wealth we're defending.
Cibo The City's bankrupt. What is there left to defend?
Duke Tell 'em it's for grain purchases. Public works on the Arno. Tell 'em anything you like Cardinal. Use your diplomatic skills!

LORENZO, DUKE *and* ALAMANNI *go*.

Vitelli I should have cut him to pieces.
Cibo Were you convinced by that?
Vitelli By what?
Cibo Lorenzo. An interesting performance.

They go.

SCENE 4

The Strozzi Palace. FILIPPO STROZZI *is alone.*

Filippo (*to the audience*) We lived in the financial centre of the world. But our decline was so rapid, our disintegration so complete, it defied our understanding. We became 'observers' at the death of our own democracy. We just stood by and we watched as our freedom disappeared. And what did I do? Filippo Strozzi, what was my role in this brief period of history? I tried, as I have always tried, to do what I thought was right. And, of course, I took great care to suit my proceedings to the time. As an honest man, I was forced to admit the failure of the republic, the stagnation of our economy, the corruption of our institutions. And, as a sensible man, I recognised our military defeat. And then, as a wise man, a noble man, I came to terms with the government of Duke Alessandro, I even argued for the disbanding of the citizen's militia. I even advocated the construction of the citadel. It just seemed to me that we needed to strengthen our defences, we needed security, stability, the rule of law. I somehow felt that a period of repressive government was necessary . . . to facilitate our recovery. Duke Alessandro knew my sympathies, I never hid them from him. He knew that I was a republican, but he tolerated me – not for what I was but for what I possessed.

Filippo Strozzi, philosopher, politician, was a man of no importance. But Filippo Strozzi international banker, that was another matter. There was a man to be treated with the utmost caution.

And what did I do?

I buried myself in my books. I returned to my business affairs. I waited for life to improve. I cultivated my love of antiquity, my devotion to Livy, to Cicero. I did the same as everyone else. I did nothing.

We were dreamers. And like all the dreamers of the past five thousand years, who've turned to dust along with their books, we failed to wash even one original stain from the face of humanity.

Oh yes, in retrospect things are always more simple, one can see the choices that were available. But human affairs are in a state of perpetual movement, always either ascending or descending. It is never easy, at the time, to know what to do.

Enter PIERO *and* LUISA.

Piero Your daughter was with Francesco Alamanni.
Filippo What's happened?
Luisa Ask your spy!
Piero I was not spying.
Luisa You were following me.
Piero Alamanni is a collaborator.
Luisa It's my life. I can do what I like.
Piero Your first obligation is to your family.
Luisa You live in a world of fantasy.
Piero You've been used Luisa. You've been made a fool of. And you're so stupid you don't even realise it.
Luisa I only went to a wedding.
Piero Do you intend to see him again?
Luisa If I want to.
Piero Do you?
Luisa (*to* FILIPPO) Tell him to leave me alone.
Piero Answer me!
Luisa I am not on trial.

Piero For God's sake, Father, tell her. Forbid her to leave the house.

Luisa Francesco Alamanni is of no interest to me. I can't be bothered to see him again.

Piero Good.

Luisa He's a pig. (*pause*) He reminds me of you.

Filippo Please, both of you.

Luisa I'm old enough to make my own decisions.

Piero Are you?

Luisa I don't need you to control my life.

Filippo That's enough! Let's just try to be reasonable.

Luisa I'm not listening to reason. I'm not giving you the chance to blind me with Socrates.

Exit LUISA.

Filippo You believe in liberty Piero, you must practise what you preach.

Piero In the home? With an irresponsible child like that? The very fact that she allows herself to be seen with Alamanni, sanctions this government!

Filippo We all sanction this government, just by being here. We pay taxes, we obey laws, we ensure that life goes on.

Piero What are you going to do?

Filippo About Luisa?

Piero Yes.

Filippo She said there was nothing in it. I believe her. (*pause*) Piero, what difference does it make? Will she be less able to find a husband because of it? Will her children respect her less? Am I even going to think of it as I kiss her good night?

Exit PIERO.

Filippo What are you doing?

Piero (*offstage*) Nothing!

PIERO *returns with a sword.*

Filippo Where are you going?

Piero Nowhere. Leave me alone!

Filippo Think, Piero, think of the consequences. What can you hope to achieve? You set family against family. Our tragedy, Piero, is our inability to speak with one voice.

Piero You are the guardian of your daughter's honour. You can't say one thing and do another.

Filippo You could be killed!

Piero I am simply doing what you always talk about.

Exit PIERO.

SCENE 5

The bank of the River Arno. Dusk. LAUDOMIA *alone. Enter* LORENZO.

Lorenzo Laudomia, what are you doing out here?

Laudomia I like to walk by the river.

Lorenzo Doesn't it occur to you that our mother might worry?

Laudomia Does it occur to you? (*pause*) From here one has a splendid view of Florence. The river. The road leading away from the city. I often come here in the evenings. I watch the passers-by. Small groups of men. Separated from their families, their homes, their possessions. This is a popular route for exiles.

Lorenzo Come home. It isn't safe for you out here.

Laudomia Stay with me Lorenzo. If you're worried about me. Stay with me.

Lorenzo No.

LORENZO *goes. Enter six* EXILES.

SONG

Exiles (*sing*)
> So good-bye to the glory of Florence
> Where everyone lives out their lives in the past
> And good-bye to the shadows of heroes
> How long, oh how long can the memory last?
>
> So good-bye you good people of Florence
> There is no-one that money, that money cannot buy
> And good-bye all you poets and painters
> For your silence, your silence said more than your lies.

Laudomia (*sings*)
> What are you crying for?
> What will your tears achieve?
> If you have cause to cry,
> You should refuse to leave.
>
> Think of those you leave behind
> Out of sight and out of mind
> They need you now,
> They won't forgive you
> If you leave now
> Their hope leaves with you.

Exiles (*sing*)

> Who, do you think you are?
> You're just a woman
> What do you think you know?
> You're just a woman
> Leave us alone
> Leave us alone.

Exiles (*sing*)

> So good-bye to the beauty of
> Florence?
> Where the bankers and bandits
> have always been friends,
> And good-bye painted whores
> and cheap virgins
> All carnivals come to an end.

Laudomia (*sings above* EXILES)

> What are you crying for?
> What will your tears achieve
> If you have cause to cry
> You should refuse to leave.
>
> Think of those you leave behind
> Out of sight and out of mind
> They need you now
> They won't forgive you
> If you leave now
> Their hope leaves with you.

The EXILES *leave.*

SCENE 6

A street. Night. PIERO *hides in doorway.* ALAMANNI *enters, drunk.* PIERO *confronts him.*

Piero Well?

Alamanni Hello.

Piero (*aside to audience*) Stupid. Formal. It was as if there was a kind of etiquette that had to be observed. We exchanged a few insults, but even then, I was never involved.

Alamanni Ready?

Piero You first.

Alamanni In your own time.

They draw their swords. PIERO *is frightened.* ALAMANNI *bursts out laughing.*

Alamanni Go on, run! Run! We didn't even meet!

ALAMANNI *turns to go.* PIERO *stabs him.* PIERO *starts to run away. A* MAN *enters, he stops* PIERO.

Man Don't move.

Pireo Please, please let me go.

Man Drop your sword.

PIERO *drops his sword.*

Piero Take my money, please.

MAN *takes* PIERO's *money.*

Man On your way.

PIERO *runs off.* MAN *approaches* ALAMANNI.

Man Can I be of any assistance?

SCENE 7

Outside a church. Early morning. An ARTIST *is painting. Enter* CARDINAL
CIBO *with* LORENZO.

Lorenzo Cardinal, your argument depends on faith. Faith is not acquired by reason.

Cibo All right. Look at the question of Eternal Life as a proposition put to a gambler. If you ask a gambler 'which is the more reasonable – to believe or not to believe in Eternal Life?' He would choose to believe.

Lorenzo Why?

Cibo Because if he wins he wins everything, and if he loses he loses nothing.

Lorenzo If a gambler used his reason, Cardinal, he would choose not to place a bet.

Cibo Where God is at stake, that choice does not exist. You make your choice for or against him by the life you lead.

Lorenzo I've made my choice Cardinal. As far as I'm concerned, christianity is an invitation to intellectual suicide.

Cibo I'm not trying to convert you.

Lorenzo No, you're just trying to take all the pleasure out of my life.

Cibo But there are other pleasures Lorenzo. Surely, even an atheist can be impressed by the outward show of the Roman Church. The magnificent cathedrals, the courtly splendour of High Mass. You're an intelligent man, don't tell me you're not moved by these things.

Lorenzo Despite rumours to the contrary Cardinal, I am not easily seduced.

Cibo You have talent Lorenzo, you have influence. Look at the way you use them.

Lorenzo The only service I could render you Cardinal would be to leave Florence, and that I refuse to do.

Cibo I'm thinking of your interest Lorenzo. Not mine.

Lorenzo I don't believe you Cardinal. You're a christian. Your every action is motivated by the promise of Eternal Life or the threat of eternal damnation. There is no room in your theology for a selfless act.

LORENZO *and* CIBO *have approached the* ARTIST, TEBALDEO.

Tebaldeo The church sponsors art. If it wished it could spend its money in another way.

Lorenzo Who are you?

Tebaldeo My name is Tebaldeo Freccia and you should listen to the Cardinal.

Lorenzo Your opinion is worthless. You have a vested interest.

Cibo What are you painting Tebaldeo?

Tebaldeo Please don't criticise it too severely. My appreciation of art is better than my practice of it.

CIBO *and* LORENZO *look at the painting.*

Lorenzo Which way up is it? Is it a landscape or a portrait?

Tebaldeo You're making fun of me.

Cibo It's a view of the Campo Santa.

Tebaldeo I'm afraid, your Eminence, that the execution falls short of the dream.

Lorenzo You paint pictures of dreams, do you? I'll get mine to pose for you sometime.

Cibo Your technique is excellent Tebaldeo.

Tebaldeo Thank you, your Eminence. My master was Andrea del Sarto, everything I know, I learned from him.

Cibo It's beautiful.

Tebaldeo I enjoy working near the church. Close to the paintings of Raphael and Buonarroti: I seem to get inspiration from them. For myself I claim no more than a mediocre talent.

Lorenzo You have delusions of adequacy my friend.

Tebaldeo Are you an artist?

Lorenzo No, but if you want inspiration, come to my house. I'll get you to paint my mistress in the nude.

Tebaldeo I'm not interested in flattering courtesans.

Lorenzo Since God took the trouble to make her, why can't you take the trouble to paint her? That's a christian argument as used by the Cardinal.

Cibo Lorenzo, you have succeeded. My patience is exhausted.

Lorenzo What's the matter Cardinal? Surely even a celibate can appreciate a nice piece of flesh.

Cibo You are beyond redemption.

Exit CARDINAL.

Lorenzo There goes the Good Shepherd, turning his back on the sheep.

Tebaldeo Clear off!

Lorenzo What's the matter?

Tebaldeo Do you know how many years I spent learning my trade?

Lorenzo I'm not interested! You paint pretty pictures of a corrupt and degenerate city and yet you refuse to paint a prostitute!

Tebaldeo I respect my art and I respect this city! I don't look at Florence the way you do. I know the affluent days are over. But great art is often the product of great suffering!

Lorenzo Well, that's wonderful. Families mourn, children starve, nations die in misery – all to excite your imagination! Go and be a parasite somewhere else!

Tebaldeo I choose to stay here.
Lorenzo This is a dangerous place for parasites.
Tebaldeo That's why I carry this stiletto.

TEBALDEO *shows his stiletto.*

Lorenzo I know you Tebaldeo. You're a friend of Piero Strozzi.
Tebaldeo I know you. Lorenzaccio.
Lorenzo Are you brave enough to use your stiletto?
Tebaldeo On anyone.
Lorenzo What if the Duke attacked you?
Tebaldeo I'd kill him.
Lorenzo Are you a republican?
Tebaldeo I'm an artist. That's all the justification I need.
Lorenzo Come to my house tomorrow. There is a painting I'd like you to do for me. A portrait.

LORENZO *goes.*

TEBALDEO'S SONG

Tebaldeo (*sings*)
> I should have smiled
> in those unhappy times:
> I had some work
> when work was hard to find,
> so why didn't I smile?

> I should have smiled.
> No-one knew my name:
> I always wanted fortune, wanted fame,
> so why didn't I smile?

> I had a simple choice:
> I could say Yes or No:
> so why didn't I say No?

SCENE 8

The Strozzi palace. Enter FILIPPO *and* LORENZO.

Filippo What's the loan for Lorenzo? For the defence of Florence? For the Citadel?
Lorenzo Are you going to pay?
Filippo How can I? How can you ask me to?

Silence.

Lorenzo Filippo, do you know where Piero is?

Filippo Why?
Lorenzo Do you know?

Silence.

Filippo He left here yesterday morning. I tried to stop him. He doesn't think.
Lorenzo He stabbed Francesco Alamanni.
Filippo Oh God.
Lorenzo It's all right. No-one's been killed. But that can't be the end of it.
Filippo Is it a crime for him to love his family? To protect his sister?
Lorenzo There are laws.
Filippo If there were laws in Florence, Alamanni would have been arrested. He'd be punished for this insult to my daughter.
Lorenzo Filippo, is the honour of your family so fragile that it can't survive the gossip of a drunk? Now please, for your own sake, think!

Enter PIERO.

Filippo Are you all right?
Piero Fine. (*Noticing* LORENZO.) What's he doing here? Why do you let him into this house?
Filippo I have my reasons.
Piero And I have a thousand reasons for throwing him out.
Filippo Haven't you done enough?
Piero What's happening to us? What has this man got to do before you see what he is? How many people must he betray? How many prisons must he fill?
Filippo You don't understand Piero.
Piero Will you understand when they come to arrest you?
Filippo Piero, listen! You've got to be careful, at least for a few days. You must hide.
Piero Hide? Why should I? The insult was in public, I answered it in public. Since when does a man hide after protecting his honour?
Filippo Listen to me.
Piero No. Stay here. Talk to your friend.
Filippo Where are you going?
Piero Out!
Filippo It isn't safe!
Piero I'm not alone. There are fifty of us, the Pazzi, the Ruccellai, the Vettori. Tell Lorenzaccio, he has reason to hide.
Filippo Piero, you don't know what you're saying! What plans have they made? What resolutions have they passed? Have they even considered the dangers? The Pazzi, the Ruccellai, they invite their friends to a conspiracy as if it were a game of cards. They talk about revolution over a glass of wine, discuss the issues while they're fencing. Politics is not a game! It's people's lives! Questions that have baffled philosophers for centuries!

MUSIC *begins*.

Do you know the meaning of the word 'Republic'? Do you know what it means to the citizen in the street? The labourer in the field? The worker at his bench? Do you have any support? Any programme? Any arms? Do you even know what it is that you want?

Piero Freedom.

Filippo What does that mean, that word? If you overthrow what exists, do you know what you'd put in its place?

Piero Whatever it is, it couldn't be worse than what we have now.

Filippo It might be Piero, if you're wrong, it might be.

PIERO *goes. Pause*.

Lorenzo Pay the loan, Filippo. Pay the loan.

SCENE 9

LORENZO's *house. Morning*. LAUDOMIA *sits in a chair, she has fallen asleep while reading a book. Silence. Enter* LORENZO.

Lorenzo You're up early.

Laudomia I fell asleep.

Lorenzo What are you reading?

He takes the book.

Laudomia *The History of Rome*.

Lorenzo My favourite book. I know a good story about Rome. Once upon a time there was a wise and virtuous Roman. He was a pacifist, and in the cause of peace he slaughtered nations. He was killed by Brutus, a man of his word who never said the same thing twice. History is ridiculous.

He hands back the book.

Laudomia I had a dream about you just now. I was alone in this room. There was a lamp on your desk, your chair was empty. I started to think of the time when we were happy. How hard you worked, how late into the night you used to read. And then I thought of you now. How you've changed. How you spend your nights, in a different way. And in my dream I cried. I heard footsteps in the corridor. I turned round. A man came in dressed in black. He had a book under his arm. It was you Lorenzo, your ghost. 'You've come home early', I said. But the ghost made no reply. He sat down at your desk. He opened a book, and I recognised the brother I used to love.

Lorenzo My dear Laudomia, it is so easy to love someone who does exactly what you want them to do.

Laudomia Is that how you interpret my dream?

Lorenzo Duke Alessandro will be here for breakfast.

Laudomia Lorenzo, why must you bring him into this house?

Lorenzo He's a friend of mine.

Laudomia Do you love him?

Lorenzo All I'm asking you to do is to be hospitable.

BINDO *and* BELLINI *enter.*

Bindo May we come in?

Laudomia Uncle Bindo and Signor Bellini, come in!

Bindo Lorenzo I heard a terrible story about you.

Lorenzo I hear them all the time.

Bindo I heard that you were challenged to a duel and you fainted.

Lorenzo Uncle Bindo, how could you believe such a thing?

Bindo Well, I didn't know what to believe. True I saw you fence in Rome. But that was a long time ago. And this life you've been leading here . . . well, it wouldn't surprise me if you'd become a coward. As well as all the other things.

Lorenzo Well the story's true Uncle. I did faint. Good morning Bellini. How's business? How's your profit?

Bellini I am a clothier not a merchant. I own looms. I have a factory in the countryside.

Lorenzo How vulgar of me to talk money.

Bindo Lorenzo, I have complete confidence in Bellini. He's a republican, a lover of liberty, and I insist that you treat him with respect! (*pause*) Now listen. You once told me that you had cultivated your friendship with the Duke as a trap. Is that true or not? Can we put our faith in you or can we not? The time has come for us to contact all the patriots in Florence, to come out into the open, to put an end, once and for all, to this Medici Duke and his tyranny! Alessandro is determined not only to destroy democracy but also to impoverish Florence. There's no individual liberty, no freedom of speech, no freedom of assembly. We've got hired mercenaries in the streets, a citadel above our heads and this so-called loan to pay for it is the last straw! What we want to know is this Lorenzo . . . are you going to use your position for us or against us?

Lorenzo What's your opinion Bellini? Speak now before he gets his breath back.

Bellini I agree with your Uncle. Every word.

Lorenzo Well, what you lack in originality, you make up for in brevity.

Bindo Lorenzo, answer the question!

Lorenzo My dear Uncle Bindo, isn't it obvious whose side I'm on? Can't you tell from the cut of my clothes and the company I keep? How could you doubt for one moment that I was not concerned for your financial affairs.

Bindo Make fun if you wish Lorenzo. But remember, money liberates man.

Enter a MANSERVANT.

Manservant My lord, the Duke of Florence is here.

Laudomia Excuse me.

Exit LAUDOMIA.

Lorenzo Show him in.

Exit MANSERVANT. *Pause. Enter* DUKE.

Lorenzo We are honoured that you should visit us.
Duke Who are these men?
Lorenzo May I present my Uncle, Signor Bindo Altoviti. Unfortunately, his long stay in Naples prevented him paying his respects to you until now.
Bindo My lord.
Lorenzo This other gentleman is Signor Baptista Bellini.
Bellini My lord.
Lorenzo Signor Bellini makes cloth but he doesn't like to be called a merchant. My Uncle makes money and he doesn't mind what you call him.

MANSERVANT *enters, he serves breakfast.*

Duke Brandy Lorenzo? Is this what you have for breakfast every morning?
Lorenzo (*to* BINDO *and* BELLINI) I'm afraid there isn't enough for all of us, gentlemen.

Exit MANSERVANT.

Bindo Well, if you'll excuse us, we must be on our way.
Lorenzo No, don't be frightened, I'm sure that everything you asked for will be granted. That is if I have any influence with the Duke.
Bindo My lord, please pay no attention to this . . .
Duke These are delicious Lorenzo. (*to* BINDO) What is it you want?
Lorenzo My Uncle has ambitions to enter the diplomatic service. He wondered if you might consider him for the court of Rome. In the whole of Florence you'll find no-one more devoted to the Medici family.
Duke Tell me Signor Bindo, do you consider our government so corrupt that we casually appoint our ambassadors over breakfast?
Lorenzo He's willing to pay.
Duke Oh well, in that case we're willing to talk. Come to my Palace tomorrow.
Bindo Thank you, my lord.
Lorenzo As for Signor Bellini who is in the cloth trade but really couldn't care less whether he sells anything, all he wants is the privilege of your arms above his door. Together with the patent of course.
Duke Would I be correct in thinking that this establishment is in the country-side?
Bellini Yes.
Duke So, what you're really asking me to do is to alienate the Florentine Guilds.
Lorenzo More wine, my lord?
Duke Come to see me tomorrow.
Bellini Thank you, my lord.

Duke You may go now, I wish to speak with Lorenzo.
Bindo Thank you Lorenzo.

> BINDO *and* BELLINI *leave.*

Duke I'm getting a lot of complaints about you Lorenzo.
Lorenzo Why my lord?
Duke Whatever the reason, the opposition to you is becoming unbearable. This relationship has got to end.
Lorenzo Why?
Duke How can I govern when my whole court is against me? I'm sorry Lorenzo, you'll have to leave Florence.
Lorenzo Why?
Duke Everyone tells me you're dangerous.
Lorenzo Do you believe that?
Duke I don't know what to believe. I'm sorry.
Lorenzo What will you do without me?
Duke I don't know.
Lorenzo I've been a good friend to you.
Duke Have you? (*pause*) All right, prove it. (*pause*) I'm in love with your sister.
Lorenzo (*laughs*) You bastard. I adore you. I've got a present for you. A young artist, a protégé of mine, I want him to paint your portrait.
Duke Don't forget your sister. That's what I really came to see you about.
Lorenzo I hope my artist will do you justice.

> *They go.*

SCENE 10

> *The* SILK MERCHANT *and the* GOLDSMITH *speak to the audience.*

Merchant We went to the fair at Monte Olivetti, but from the moment we arrived I could see that my friend here was not very happy.
Goldsmith I wouldn't say that. It was a religious festival. We made the pilgrimage. Our sins were remitted. So, it wasn't entirely a waste of time.
Merchant You weren't happy though were you.
Goldsmith Neither of us was really. We'd taken all sorts of things along, cups, crucifixes, things like that. There was hardly anyone there.
Merchant They were in church.
Goldsmith Yes. Anyway we set up, and before we knew where we were Piero Strozzi arrived. He said he was looking for the Vettori family.
Merchant They were in church.
Goldsmith. So you said. Anyway, while we were waiting I took the chance to pass the time of day with him. As it happened I had something he might have been interested in. I'd brought along some medallions. One of them

had the head of Demosthenes on. And what with him being a student, I thought he might be interested.

Merchant And he was.

Goldsmith Yes he was.

Merchant Didn't buy it though, did he.

Goldsmith No.

Merchant Nearly.

Goldsmith Yes. As a matter of fact he had his hand in his purse when it happened.

Merchant A soldier came up. He got arrested.

Goldsmith Yes.

Merchant You were furious.

Goldsmith Who wouldn't be? First sale of the day.

Merchant That was before you knew though, wasn't it.

Goldsmith Before either of us knew. I stood up for him though. I told this soldier, 'Piero Strozzi is one of the finest young men in Florence'.

Merchant Then what happened?

Goldsmith You were there. Captain Vitelli arrived on the scene. We were lucky not to find ourselves arrested. Things got very nasty after that. Vitelli said he had a warrant from the Duke. Piero Strozzi said he didn't recognise his authority.

Merchant They took him away though didn't they.

Goldsmith Yes. And he started shouting things like 'This is what the citadel is for' . . .

Merchant (*animated*) 'This is what the soldiers are for', 'This is oppression, force, tyranny', 'If they can arrest me they can arrest you', 'My freedom is your freedom'. (*pause*) He wanted us to help didn't he.

Goldsmith Yes.

Merchant We didn't though, did we.

Goldsmith No.

Merchant 'Cos Captain Vitelli threatened to take our licences away.

Goldsmith That wasn't the reason.

Merchant Wasn't it?

Goldsmith No. What happened was this. I said 'What had he done?' I demanded to be told. And then Vitelli said 'Piero Strozzi almost killed a man'. So I said 'Oh' 'Oh' sort of ambiguously.

Merchant Then Captain Vitelli said 'If you don't clear off, I'll take your licence away'.

Goldsmith Yes. But that was after we found out he was a criminal.

Merchant So we went home.

Goldsmith We didn't know what to do. I mean all we were interested in was the festival, the fair.

Merchant And selling our goods.

Goldsmith Well, that's what we were there for.

SONG

Goldsmith (*sings*)
> Everyone's in trouble
> From the pauper to the king
> They all need assistance
> so don't try to do a thing.

Merchant (*sings*)
> That's good advice, I feel quite sure:
> we've all got trouble, we don't need more.

Merchant (*sings*)
> If you see a drowning man,
> he should have learnt to swim.
> Don't you lend a helping hand:
> he'll only pull you in.

Goldsmith (*sings*)
> That's good advice, I won't forget:
> you lend a hand, your feet get wet.

Goldsmith (*sings*)
> If a beggar asks for bread,
> don't let him have a crumb.
> It pays you to pretend, my friend,
> you're blind, you're deaf and dumb.

Merchant (*sings*)
> Such good advice I can't ignore:
> the act of friendship makes men poor.

Merchant/Goldsmith (*sing*)
> All we want's a quiet life,
> a happy home, a loving wife,
> a paradise of hearts and flowers:
> you've got your problems; we've got ours.

SCENE 11

The DUKE's *Palace. The* DUKE *is having his portrait painted by* TEBALDEO.
CAPTAIN VITELLI *paces up and down.*

Duke Captain Vitelli, you're upsetting my concentration.

Vitelli My lord, soldiers have got to eat. What can I do with 'em if they're half-starving?

Duke How's Piero?
Vitelli Him? He's all right.
Duke Good. So long as he's comfortable.
Vitelli What about the money!?
Duke Wait and see.
Vitelli How long?

Enter LORENZO.

Lorenzo How's the masterpiece? What are you doing half-naked?
Duke The artist wanted it like this. He said it would lend a classical effect.
Lorenzo You have a keen sense of humour Tebaldeo. Do you like your new
    patron?
Tebaldeo An artist is like any other worker. He can't live on thin air.

LORENZO *picks up the* DUKE'*s chain mail.*

Lorenzo (*to the* DUKE) I've never known you take this off before. It's beautiful.
Duke The finest steel wire.
Lorenzo So light. So strong. There isn't another one like it in all Europe.
    (*to* TEBALDEO) The sharpest blade couldn't pierce it. Nothing will get
    through there. Not even a stiletto. (*to* DUKE) Aren't you afraid without
    it my lord?
Duke Not in here.
Lorenzo No. I suppose you've only got the painter to worry about. And art is
    above politics, it rarely bites the hand that feeds it. Despite appearances.
    (*To* TEBALDEO) You're like me Tebaldeo, too sensitive to carry a sword.
Vitelli My orders.
Lorenzo Vitelli, if you stand any closer to the Duke, you'll be in the picture.
    (*To* TEBALDEO) You're doing well my friend, the Duke looks like a
    philosopher. No doubt your friends will be very pleased by your attention
    to detail. Wait here. I'll go and get my guitar. I'll inspire you with a song
    about thin air.

LORENZO *attempts to leave with the chain mail.*

Vitelli Lorenzo! (VITELLI *beckons* LORENZO *to him.*) I looked up Sybarite in
    the dictionary. You are one.
Lorenzo I looked you up in the dictionary Vitelli. You weren't there.

LORENZO *goes. He takes the chain mail with him.*

Tebaldeo Please excuse me, my lord, I can't work any more today.
Duke May I look?
Tebaldeo If you want.
Vitelli (*looking out of the window*) What's Lorenzo doing out there? He said
    he was going to get his guitar. He's looking into the well.
Duke Give me my clothes. (*pause*) Where's my chain mail?
Tebaldeo Lorenzo was holding it.

Duke Where did he put it?

They search.

Vitelli It's not here.
Duke It must be.

Enter LORENZO *with his guitar.*

Lorenzo What's the matter?
Tebaldeo I'm cleaning my brushes.
Lorenzo What temperament! What genius!
Duke Where did you put my chain mail? We can't find it.
Lorenzo I put it back where it was. No I didn't, I gave it to Vitelli.
Vitelli You didn't give it to me.
Lorenzo No? Can't remember. Let's think. I was over here. Can't find it. I
found my guitar though.
Vitelli Where was it? At the bottom of the well? I saw you from the window.
Lorenzo You do take an extraordinary interest in my life Vitelli. I was having
a spit. A harmless pleasure. I suppose that's another of my activities that
fails to meet with your approval.
Duke Lorenzo, what have you done with it?
Lorenzo (*smiles*) I've got a message from my sister.
Duke (*smiles*) All right. Let's go where we can talk.

LORENZO *and* DUKE *go.*

Vitelli Not happy. Where was he standing? Why spit? No sense in it.
Tebaldeo There's a lot of things in life that don't make sense.
Vitelli You're not paid to think.

SCENE 12

CARDINAL CIBO *and* CAPTAIN VITELLI *on stage. A naked* MAN *sits between
them. This scene is a ceremony where they dress the man in the garments of
the Emperor Charles the Fifth. Some of the following lines are spoken,
some are sung.*

Cibo Divine reason, which is beyond our understanding, determines the
Eternal Law by which the entire universe is governed. Angels, men, the
animal and vegetable kingdoms, material nature, both in the celestial
and terrestrial spheres—all these are subject to its immutable necessity.
Vitelli The only way to establish any kind of order is to found a monarchical
government; for where the body of the people is so thoroughly corrupt
that the laws are powerless for restraint, it becomes necessary to establish
some superior power which, with a royal hand, and with full and absolute
authority, may put a curb upon the excessive ambition and corruption
of the powerful.

Cibo For man there is a twofold jurisdiction, the Eternal Law and the human law. Human law is subordinate to Eternal Law, but give to each its due and all will be in harmony.

Vitelli There are two ways of contending, one in accordance with the laws, the other by force. The first of which is proper to men, the second to beasts. But since the first method is often ineffectual, it becomes necessary to resort to the second. A prince should therefore understand how to use well both the man and the beast.

Cibo Man is bound to obey man in those external actions which are performed by the body. The subject is bound to obey his superior within the range covered by his authority. For example, a soldier is bound to obey his general in those matters which pertain to the conduct of war. . . .

Vitelli From this there arises the question, whether it is better to be loved more than feared.

Cibo . . . a slave his master in the performance of his servile duty . . .

Vitelli The reply is that one ought to be both loved and feared.

Cibo . . . the son his father.

Vitelli But as it is difficult for the two to go together, it is much safer to be feared than loved.

Cibo/Vitelli For the minds of men are timorous, their devices are prone to fail: they are voluble, dissemblers, anxious to avoid danger, and covetous of gain.

Vitelli The order is eternal, it is immutable.

Cibo It accords with the will of God.

Cibo/Vitelli And the alternative is chaos, the cosmic anarchy that was before creation.

Charles Lord God. I know that time will pass, and I along with it. But give me time to bring my country peace. How lovely is peace! How hard to achieve! In troubled and uncertain times, please help thy servant Charles, King of the Romans, elected Roman Emperor, semper Augustus, King of Spain, Sicily, Jerusalem, the Balearic Islands, the Canary Islands, the Indies and the mainland on the far side of the Atlantic. Archduke of Austria, Duke of Burgundy, Brabant, Styria, Corinthia, Cornolia, Luxemburg, Limburg, Athens and Patras, Count of Hapsburg, Flanders and Tyrol, Count Palatine of Burgundy, Hainault, Pfirt, Roussillon, Landgrave of Alsace, Count of Swabia, Lord of Asia and Africa. Help me Lord.

SCENE 13

A public place. LORENZO *and* FILIPPO *enter.*

Filippo Lorenzo, I have watched you. I have seen you impersonate the very darkest side of human nature and I have understood. But now let the man replace the actor. Piero is in prison.

Lorenzo I know.

Filippo Is that your reply?

Lorenzo Tell me what you want. Then I'll reply.

Filippo I want him released. I want you to act. I want to do something myself. Please tell me now, because now is the time for us to do it. (*pause*) Lorenzo, everywhere you go, people abuse you, they treat you with contempt. But despite everything I've kept my door open to you, my heart, my hand open to you. Tell me that I have not been wrong. Speak to me. Tell me about the other Lorenzo, the one who loves his country, devotes himself to his friends. You spoke to me once about him, and I believed you.

Lorenzo I remember . . . just about.

Filippo You made promises to me that would have been binding on God himself. And that's why I received you. When everything you did contradicted my faith in you. I called you still by the sacred name of 'friend'. In order to believe you I made myself deaf. In order to believe you I made myself blind. My children distrusted me because I shook your hand. Be honest with me Lorenzo, as I have been with you. Act! You are a young man. Tell me what I should do. Tell me, and I will do it!

Lorenzo My dear Filippo, stay home.

Filippo I can't!

Lorenzo There are many devils Filippo, and the one tempting you now is the most dangerous.

Filippo What do you mean?

Lorenzo Liberty. Patriotism. Human happiness.

Filippo I don't understand.

Lorenzo Do you really want just to release your son from prison? Isn't there something else you want? Something bigger?

Filippo This injustice to my family could be the spark that starts an uprising.

Lorenzo Beware of yourself, Filippo, you are thinking of the well-being of humanity.

Filippo Oh Lorenzo, are you corrupted on the inside as well?

Lorenzo I'm going to kill Alessandro.

Filippo I don't believe you.

Lorenzo In a few days there will no longer be a Duke of Florence.

Filippo If you mean what you say, why am I wrong to think of freedom? If you kill Alessandro, everything is possible. But Lorenzo, the ground must be prepared. Who have you told?

Lorenzo Filippo, be careful, be careful, your sixty years of virtue are too valuable to risk on the throw of a dice. (*pause*) No matter how I might appear to you now, I was once honourable. I had faith in humanity as a martyr has faith in God. But for twenty years my life was leading, inevitably, to this moment. I was in Rome. At night. Sitting in the ruins of the Colosseum. Suddenly I stood up, stretched my arms towards heaven, and swore that I would kill a tyrant! I don't know what happened, how I felt. Perhaps it's how someone feels when they fall in love, I don't know. There was a time, yes, when I wanted to be good, but from that moment, to my everlasting sorrow, I wanted to be great! And you will never know, unless you are mad, the ecstasy that possessed me. I was Brutus. I wanted to act alone. I wanted to kill the tyrant. To carry my bloody sword to the people. To let the sight, the smell of the oppressor's blood inflame the brains of tired speech-makers. (*pause*) It wasn't easy with Alessandro, first of all I had to win his confidence. In order to please him I became a clown, a wit, a coward. I was vicious, ruthless, the most charming of all procurors. We drank together, gambled together, made love together . . . what does that matter? All you need know is that I succeeded in my task. Alessandro trusts me.

Filippo If what you say is true you could indeed be our Brutus. But Lorenzo the conditions must be right, the timing must be right. These are political questions. They are absolutely crucial to our success.

Lorenzo Oh, Filippo, you're a good man, you've led a virtuous life. But you have seen only the surface while I have explored the depths. The fault of books and of historians is that they depict men different from what they are. A man can live in a city all his life and see only the parks and the palaces, but what does he know if he never enters the brothels and the gambling dens? (*pause*) This is my advice, Filippo, if you want to save your son, keep quiet, stay indoors and pay the loan.

Filippo Are you asking me to finance the citadel?

Lorenzo If you want your son released from prison, yes.

Filippo And my honour, what happens to that?

Lorenzo If you are concerned for your fellow man and you want to do something for humanity. You're a fool, because it won't be long before you discover you stand alone.

Filippo No. People are not governed solely by self-interest. There are such things as human virtues.

Lorenzo Dreams. I've stopped dreaming. I've woken up. I've seen life, and life is ugly.

Filippo The four cardinal virtues, are they dreams? Wisdom, courage, temperance, justice, men have died for these things, Lorenzo.

Lorenzo I am Lorenzaccio. Have you seen me as I walk through the streets of this city? The children don't throw mud at me. No one slips poison into my cup. The beds of young girls are still wet from my sweat and yet their fathers do not attack me as I leave. In return for a few miserable pieces of gold a loving mother will offer her daughter to me. And when I smile it's just to suffocate a scream inside.

Filippo Lorenzo, don't despise the weak.

Lorenzo I could have cried for the first virgin that I abused until that moment when she began to laugh. Filippo, I had barely taken the first steps of my journey when I saw that everyone was doing what I was doing. The whole of society lifted its veil to show me a price stamped on its forehead. I saw men as they really are. And I asked myself 'Who am I doing this for?' I would go for a walk around the streets of Florence, look at a stranger and ask myself 'When I have done this act, will he benefit by it?' I watched the republicans in their studies, I visited the shops, I listened to people talking, I saw the effect of tyranny upon them. I was always looking, waiting, waiting for humanity to show me one honest face.

Filippo Lorenzo if you see in man only that which is despicable then with all my heart I pity you. I know that evil exists, but not without good. Shadows exist but not without light.

Lorenzo I don't despise men. I am quite aware that there are some good ones. But what cause are they serving? What do they do? How do they act? What use is their conscience if it doesn't determine their actions? No, people will not benefit from what I have to do. They will not even understand it.

Filippo Lorenzo this murder can save you. It will be an exorcism.

Lorenzo Too late. Corruption was once merely a cloak for me. Now it becomes part of me. Take my advice Filippo, do not serve your country.

Filippo Lorenzo you chose evil means to serve a virtuous end. But that is not the only path available.

Lorenzo Take whatever path you like, you still have to deal with men.

Filippo Now come on, that's ridiculous. You're indulging yourself.

Lorenzo I'll take a bet with you Filippo. I am going to kill Alessandro. Once he is dead anything will be possible. The republicans can take power if they act as they should. I bet Filippo, that nobody does a thing!

Filippo If you believe that, why kill the Duke?

Lorenzo Why?!!

Filippo If you believe that this murder is futile, why do it?

Lorenzo Filippo, look at me! Look at what is left of me! I am a shadow. The ghost of what I was. Do you want me to break the only thread which joins my heart to the heart I used to have? Don't you understand? This murder is all that there is left for me. It's the only thing I've got to hold on to. Without that my life means nothing. Filippo, if I could, if only I could for one moment, forget what I know, forget what I've seen, forget what I've become, then yes, I might spare the Duke. But my dear Filippo I enjoy my corruption! I enjoy being Lorenzaccio! And if there is anything in me that you should respect, then it is this murder, if only because you could not do it yourself! But that's enough. I'm tired of the sound of words. In a few days, in a very few days the world will know who I am and who he was. I shall kill Alessandro, whether men understand or not. Whether they act or not. And I shall have said all that I have to say.

END OF ACT 1

ACT 2
SCENE 14

LORENZO's house. Late at night, very dark. LORENZO *and* SCORONCONCOLO *are fencing.* SCORONCONCOLO *is played by the actor who plays the* MAN *in the Prologue.*

Lorenzo Kill him! Kill him!
Scoronconcolo Assassin!
Lorenzo Hold him! Pin him down!
Scoronconcolo Help! Help! Mercy!
Lorenzo Revenge!
Scoronconcolo Agh!
Lorenzo Revenge! Revenge!

> *The lights come up. We see that* LORENZO *and* SCORONCONCOLO *are 'acting'.*

1st Voice (*off*) Do you know what time it is?
2nd Voice (*off*) Keep it down. People are trying to sleep.
Lorenzo Revenge!
Scoronconcolo Help! He's attacking me!
1st Voice (*off*) For Christ's sake! Not again!
Lorenzo Revenge!
3rd Voice (*off*) Shut up!
Lorenzo Kill him! Stab him! Rip him open!

> SCORONCONCOLO *collapses.*

Scoronconcolo Enough, my lord, no more.
Lorenzo Come on! Come on!
Scoronconcolo I'm exhausted.
Lorenzo Get up!
Scoronconcolo I can't.
Lorenzo Stand up you coward! Stand up! Grab him! Slice him! Pull out his guts! Poke your hand in! Explore him! Come on! Come on!
Scoronconcolo You don't like your neighbours, do you?
Lorenzo What?
Scoronconcolo Do you remember the first time?
Lorenzo Eh?
Scoronconcolo They came out in the street. They knocked on the door. Not now. You could kill twenty men in here. Roll their heads round the floor. Throw their limbs out the window. Your neighbours wouldn't get out of bed.

Lorenzo Are you bored with our game?

Scoronconcolo If you have an enemy, my lord, tell me.

Lorenzo There's no enemy.

Scoronconcolo You're getting thin. You don't laugh any more. Tell me his name. I have the answer here.

SCORONCONCOLO *presents his stiletto.*

Lorenzo How often have you used it?

Scoronconcolo Often.

LORENZO *examines the stiletto.*

Lorenzo Do they scream?

Scoronconcolo Not always. Sometimes they're too frightened.

Lorenzo What happens?

Scoronconcolo Nothing. They just receive death.

Lorenzo Quietly?

Scoronconcolo Not a sound.

Lorenzo Do they . . . do they bleed much?

Scoronconcolo Oh yes.

Lorenzo What about . . . what about afterwards. How do you feel?

Scoronconcolo Depends.

Lorenzo Yes. I do have an enemy. But for him I won't use a blade that has been used on another man.

LORENZO *returns the stiletto.*

Lorenzo Do you love me Scoronconcolo?

Scoronconcolo For you I would nail Christ back on the cross.

Lorenzo I'm going to kill my enemy here in this room. He'll come to the door. I'll open it. He'll smile. I'll smile. Perhaps . . . ? No. I'll take his cloak.

Scoronconcolo If he's wearing one.

Lorenzo I'll offer him wine. Get him to sit down. Yes.

Scoronconcolo My lord, let me do it. It's my trade.

Lorenzo No. I just want you to be here, that's all. If the first blow doesn't kill him. Hold him. Hold his hands. That's all I want you to do. Do you understand? It has to be me.

Scoronconcolo When?

Lorenzo Soon. Take this money.

Scoronconcolo I don't need it.

Lorenzo Take it. There's fifty florins. Speak to no-one.

Scoronconcolo You can trust me. I don't need money.

Lorenzo Take it – then I'll believe you.

Scoronconcolo Thank you.

LORENZO *addresses* SCORONCONCOLO *as the* MAN *in the Prologue.*

Lorenzo That was what we did. You enjoyed that didn't you.

SCENE 15

The Bargello. PIERO *on stage alone. The* COMPANY *sing off stage.*

PRISONERS' SONG

Prisoners (*sing*)
What do you want me to do?
What do you want me to say?
How do I know if you won't tell me?
Where do you want me to sign?

When I get out of here,
I will remember:
However long it takes,
I will remember.

I won't forget
One line on any face:
I won't forget
One part of any day.

Piero (*sings*)
I can see now
Nothing that I couldn't see before:
But I am changing.
I am learning
Everything I always learnt before,
But in a new way.
I am learning,
Though they keep me on my own,
I know I'm not alone – we're not alone.
We are learning,
Just by being here,
No longer in the mind
But in the body.

Prisoners (*sing*)
Is it morning?
I see daylight.
Can you hear me?
Are you all right?
Are you frightened?
Don't be frightened.
Don't be frightened.

PIERO *walks forward as if leaving prison. Enter* TEBALDEO *and a* SERVANT. *The* SERVANT *carries a coat.*

Piero Where's my father? Why isn't he here to meet me?

Silence.

Servant He's gone.
Piero Where?

The SERVANT *hopes that* TEBALDEO *will reply. Pause.*

Servant Venice. Yesterday. He closed everything down, the house, the bank, he took a few servants, he left most of us here.
Piero What happened?
Tebaldeo Luisa.
Piero What?
Tebaldeo She's dead.
Piero Oh God.
Tebaldeo She was poisoned. We think it was the Alamanni family. We don't know.
Piero Oh God.
Servant He took everything, furniture, books, wagons, horses. He put the body in a carriage, following behind the caravan. He didn't want her to be buried in Florence.
Tebaldeo (*to* PIERO) I'm sorry.

The SERVANT *put the coat over* PIERO'*s shoulders.*

Servant I know this is a terrible moment but I must ask you, I just don't know what to do. My family slept on your doorstep last night. We've got nowhere to go. There's no work anywhere. I don't know who to turn to.
Piero I'm sorry, I can't help you.
Servant Have you any suggestions?
Piero In prison there are men who have no hope, they are broken, totally. And now this, here, on the outside.
Servant Can you help?
Piero (*to* TEBALDEO) Did my father say he was going to meet anyone? Did he mention the exiles?
Tebaldeo He didn't say a word.
Piero I must go to Venice.
Servant What about my family?
Piero I've got no money. I need a horse. I haven't even got the money to pay for it.
Servant Please my lord. How am I going to feed my children?
Piero What can I do?
Servant My children must eat!
Piero I'll be back. I promise you, I'll be back.

PIERO *and* TEBALDEO *leave.* TEBALDEO *contemplates giving money to the* SERVANT. *The* SERVANT *leaves.*

SCENE 16

LORENZO'*s house.* LAUDOMIA *is reading a letter.* LORENZO *watches her.*

Laudomia Peculiar handwriting.

Lorenzo What do you think?

Laudomia Very nice.

Lorenzo What does it say?

Laudomia The Duke thinks I'm going to jump into bed with him.

Lorenzo (*laughs*) Ridiculous. Are you going to reply?

Laudomia Yes. I'll tell him I can't wait.

Lorenzo I don't believe you!

Laudomia Why not? This is what I've been waiting for. I'll write to him, arrange to meet him and then, at last, I can talk to him.

Lorenzo What about?

Laudomia He's in love with me. With a little skill, a little care, who knows what influence I might have?

Lorenzo He won't listen.

Laudomia He listens to a lot of people. I've got a tremendous advantage over them.

Lorenzo He's not interested in your mind.

Laudomia Not yet. But this is a chance. An opportunity. It's too good to miss.

Lorenzo You can't change him.

Laudomia How do we know until we try?

Lorenzo He's a tyrant. He's corrupt. He can't be anything else.

Laudomia People can change Lorenzo. Look at yourself.

Lorenzo No! I respect your motives, but it won't work!

Laudomia If you care about anything at all you must at least let me try.

Lorenzo I'm going to kill Alessandro.

Laudomia What?

Lorenzo Remember the ghost? He's come back.

Laudomia You're mad.

Lorenzo That's right. I am. I am Brutus. I'm going to kill our Caesar.

Laudomia Insane.

Lorenzo Write the letter Laudomia. Tell him you're going to meet him. Then leave the rest to my insanity.

Laudomia If you think you're going to kill Alessandro, you have no idea what's happening in this country. He's a puppet. If he goes he'll be replaced. Look, let me talk to him. At least we know him. We know his weaknesses.

Lorenzo He's not a fool.

Laudomia But if you kill him, the next Duke may be worse.

Lorenzo I want to kill him!

Laudomia It doesn't matter what you want! The point is to change society.

Lorenzo (*laughs*) Oh my sweet, sweet sister. I used to think like that once. I used to care about my fellow man. Politics once meant something to me. Not any more. As far as I'm concerned people get the government they deserve. And I reached that conclusion reluctantly through experience. I shall kill Alessandro because I have to, because if I did not kill him, my life would be an absurdity!

Laudomia What about my life? If I let this opportunity go, then my life doesn't make sense!

Lorenzo Please! All I'm asking you to do is to help me!

Laudomia No! If I'm not given the chance to do something then I refuse to write your letter.

Lorenzo Take it. Write the letter. I am supremely confident that you will fail. Take your golden opportunity. Meet the Duke. I'll be outside the door, waiting.

LAUDOMIA *goes.*

Lorenzo (*to the audience*) words, words, everlasting words. And if there was a God, he'd look down on us and laugh. The chatter of feeble humanity. We kill dead bodies, we break in open doors.

MIDDLE-LOGUE

The MAN *from the Prologue appears.*

Lorenzo (*continues*) And who was I, above all men, to behave as if I was the instrument of destiny? What had this man ever done to me that I had the right to kill him? He had been cruel to others but to me he had been kind. Generous, in his own way. I could have stayed at home, I could have led a quiet life. He would never have come to look for me. And yet I travelled, I came all the way to Florence to seek him out. I was not devout, there was no God in which I believed, but in all sincerity, I hoped that he would say a prayer before he came to visit me. I wanted to go to an inn. I could have emptied a flagon of wine just then. But no, I did not dare to drink. I had the strangest desire to dance. If I could have let myself go I would have performed a wild carnival dance along the street. Have you ever felt like that?

Man Yes.

Lorenzo Did you feel like that when you decided to meet me?

Man No. Not the same.

Lorenzo Is that your best suit?

Man (*embarrassed*) No.

LORENZO *notices the flower in the lapel of the* MAN'*s best suit.*

Lorenzo Did you pick that flower especially for me?

The MAN *laughs, embarrassed.*

How fragile is the force of destiny. You can deliberate, you can choose. But having chosen you cannot retrace your steps. And when you complete this action, you abandon everything! As I did.

MAN *disappears.*

END OF MIDDLE-LOGUE

LORENZO'S SONG

Lorenzo (*sings*)
    Anything else?
    What have I forgotten?
    Wine? Food?
    It won't matter if he screams.
    Key? Sword?
    The lamp beside the bed?
    What will he wear?
    He'll be alone:
    Don't keep me waiting.

    The room must be prepared.
    There must be flowers everywhere.
    And silk sheets on the bed:
    It must be perfect.

    And when I've done it,
    My life is over:
    I'm in hell:
    It will be perfect.

SCENE 17

Venice. FILIPPO STROZZI *and three monks at* LUISA's *tomb.*

1st Monk Fac, quaesumus, Domine, hanc cum ancilla tua defuncta misericordiam, ut factorum suorum in poenis non recipiat vicem, quae tuam in votis tenuit voluntatem, ut sicut hic eam vera fides junxit fidelium turmis; ita illic eam tua miseratio societ angelicis choris. Per Christum Dominum nostrum.

All Monks Amen.

They make the sign of the cross.

1st Monk Requiem aeternam dona ei Domine.
All Monks Et lux perpetua luceat ei.
1st Monk Requiescat in pace.
All Monks Amen.

PIERO *enters. The chant continues underneath the scene.*

Piero (*whispers*) Father. (*pause*) I'm sorry.
Filippo I feel so desolate.

FILIPPO *cries.* PIERO *embraces him.*

Piero Now we've got to do something. We must.
Filippo Yes.

FILIPPO *begins to recover.*

Piero Prison has changed me Father. There are no more illusions. Duke Alessandro is weak. In Florence, at least eighty of the great families oppose him. There are all the exiles. All these forces, just waiting for leadership. That's the only thing that's holding them back. The time is ripe for us. I can feel it.
Filippo Yes. Yes. I know.
Piero Come with me to Mirandola. The exiles are gathering an army together. They are hiring soldiers. If you agree to lead them they will march on Florence.
Filippo No. We must appeal to the Pope. We must send a delegation.
Piero That's not enough.
Filippo I've already written to the Emperor.
Piero Come to Mirandola. You're the most respected man in Florence. If you lead the exiles, others will join. We may even get support from the King of France. We could attack at night. Surprise the guards. If we take the citadel it will all be over.
Filippo You are asking me to take up arms against my country. To defy the law.
Piero Yes!
Filippo Civilisation depends upon the rule of law. If we destroy respect for law society collapses and we open the door to anarchy.
Piero History is made by men who break laws.
Filippo Piero you are young. You've learned words from me.
Piero Are you going to act or not?
Filippo I can't do what you ask.
Piero Is that your answer?
Filippo Tell the exiles that Filippo Strozzi has no room in his life for more sorrow.
Piero Tell them yourself. Tell them you choose to retire into solitude when the world is in flames!
Filippo My God, what do you know about solitude?

Piero I was a prisoner. I am now an exile.

Filippo I didn't know.

Piero I am ashamed of you. All that you have ever done, with all your learning, is to enrich your own vocabulary. Stay here, stay here with the other old men. Enjoy your misery in the comfort and prosperity of Venice. You've had your life!

Filippo Where are you going?

Piero Back to Florence! To break the law! In the University of Bologna, the students, are not afraid of the future, they can't afford to be! Their lives will never be determined by a translator of Latin!

PIERO *goes. The* MONKS *finish their chant.*

1st Monk Anima ejus, et animae omnium fidelium defunctorum, per misericordiam Dei requiescant in pace.

All Monks Amen.

SCENE 18

A square. Night. The GOLDSMITH *and* SILK MERCHANT *enter. They sit at a table. Silence.*

Goldsmith I don't know.

Merchant Nor do I.

Silence.

Goldsmith What's your opinion of my wife? Be honest.

Merchant Well . . .

Goldsmith Go on . . .

Merchant Well . . .

Goldsmith Frivolous? Yes that just about sums her up. When I got home last night she had pink hair. Pink. (*pause*) Blue eyelids, orange face, pink hair. (*pause*) Not natural is it?

Merchant Is it the fashion?

Goldsmith Do you know how much she costs me each week? Beautifying water, perfume, coloured cream, false hair, dresses, French fashions, Spanish soap. I can't keep up with it. (*pause*) I wouldn't mind if I could see an improvement.

Merchant You get variety.

Enter MAN *with drinks.*

Goldsmith Who's doing the honours?

Merchant Whose turn is it?

Goldsmith Who got 'em last night?

Merchant Where were we last night?

Goldsmith I'll get 'em tomorrow.

MERCHANT *pays* MAN, *Exit* MAN.

Goldsmith Good health.

They drink.

Goldsmith Venice. That's where we ought to be. Can't fail. Know why? Access to the sea. Cheap imports. Raw materials. Anyone could make money in Venice. Investment, expansion, competition, prices down, production up, more profit, more investment. And round it goes. Poetry.

Merchant Florence was like that once.

Goldsmith Now look at it. Waste of time getting up in the mornings. I stand outside my shop, I ask myself, 'What does it all mean?' 'What am I doing here?'

Merchant You're protecting your property. Keeping the thieves off.

Goldsmith The answer to a prayer. Insurance!

Merchant Insurance?

Goldsmith Liquidise my assets.

Merchant They'd put the premiums up.

Goldsmith Who cares? I'd be gone.

Merchant What about the shop?

Goldsmith Burn it down. Fire and theft.

Merchant On the same night? They'll investigate. You'd get caught. Where's your policy? Check the small print. There's sure to be a clause against it. What am I saying? It's a crime. Fraud. Pull yourself together. You're a respectable businessman. A law-abiding citizen. You don't have a criminal mentality.

Goldsmith One more day like this. Just one more.

Enter LORENZO. *He stands in a corner of the acting area and begins to throw stones up at the window. They watch him.*

Goldsmith If he's not careful, he'll break that window.

Lorenzo Signor Pazzi! Hello!

Voice (*off*) Yes? What is it? What do you want?

Lorenzo Prepare for tomorrow. The Duke will be killed tonight.

Voice (*off*) What are you talking about? Who's going to kill him?

Lorenzo Lorenzo de' Medici.

Voice (*off*) Lorenzaccio, is that you? You're drunk. Come up and join us.

Lorenzo There's no time. I'm going to kill the Duke.

Voice (*off*) And I'm going to marry the Pope! Clear off!

MERCHANT *and* GOLDSMITH *look at each other, take a drink, resume watching.* LORENZO *crosses to another corner.*

Lorenzo Signor Vettori! Signor Vettori! Hello!

Voice (*off*) Who's calling? Who is it?

Lorenzo I've come to tell you that Duke Alessandro will be killed tonight. Prepare yourself. Make your plans for tomorrow.

Voice (*off*) Who told you this? Who's going to kill him?
Lorenzo It doesn't matter. Prepare for tomorrow.
Voice (*off*) Who are you? Tell me your name?
Lorenzo I can't.
Voice (*off*) Lunatic!

LORENZO *crosses to another corner.*

Goldsmith Terrible. These youngsters can't take their drink.

They watch LORENZO.

Lorenzo Hello! Anyone there? Signor Corsini! Hello!
Voice (*off*) What's going on?
Voice (*off*) Lorenzaccio you're a pest.
Lorenzo Listen to me.
Voice (*off*) Do you want a bucket of water on your head? Clear off!

LORENZO *turns to face the* MERCHANTS.

Merchant Oh no. Here he comes.
Goldsmith Ignore him.

GOLDSMITH *whistles a tune.* LORENZO *stands by their table.*

Goldsmith No parties tonight, sir?
Lorenzo They don't believe me.
Goldsmith No? Must have our little joke, eh sir? What it is to be young?
Lorenzo They don't believe me.
Merchant If I were you sir, I'd get an early night.
Lorenzo I knew it was a waste of time.

LORENZO *goes.*

Goldsmith I don't know.
Merchant Nor do I.

SONG

Merchant (*sings*)
> What a lovely night:
> such a perfect way
> to end a lousy day.

Goldsmith (*sings*)
> Good night, my friend:
> it is time for us
> to wend our weary way.

Merchant/Goldsmith (*sing*)
>   Good night, my friend:
>   it is time for us
>   to wend our weary way.

Merchant (*sings*)
>   All the trouble we go through,
>   and the worrying we do!

Goldsmith (*sings*)
>   You understand
>   that the businessman
>   is the one who carries the can:

Merchant (*sings*)
>   but then again
>   philosophically
>   we spend another night.

Goldsmith (*sings*)
>   Back home to face the wife.
Merchant (*sings*)
>   What a satisfactory life!
Goldsmith (*sings*)
>   Good night!
Merchant (*sings*)
>   Good night!

They go.

SCENE 19

The DUKE'*s Palace.* DUKE ALESSANDRO *is getting dressed.*

Duke (*to the audience*) No chain mail. I still went out. Dressed to kill I made the perfect victim. I knew precisely what my position was. I was a puppet. Caught between two irreconcilable forces.

On the one hand the republicans were against me, they were historically obliged to challenge me. They had economic power, they needed political power. And on the other hand I had to contend with the Pope and the Emperor. They had appointed me to safeguard their imperial interests. So what should I have done? Should I have served my masters or my subjects?

If I had tried to be a benevolent ruler, if I had given the republicans what they wanted; individual freedom, democratic government, then, at the very least, their first act would have been to banish me from Florence.

If I had tried to govern as my ancestors did. If I had attempted the same grandeur, the same enlightenment, I would have made this city bankrupt overnight.

The conditions had changed, it was no longer possible to recreate the past.

Whichever way I turned I was tightening the noose around my own neck.

I did not choose to be Duke Alessandro, it was never my ambition to seek political power. But since I had it, no matter how limited, no matter how temporary, I was determined to enjoy it totally.

I had no idea what constituted human happiness, but in the time given to me I simply wanted the maximum pleasure.

We have one life that is the only thing we have. And life is utterly and completely meaningless, it was my good fortune to realise that when I was young. Why should I care about history? Let history take care of itself.

The end was inevitable, the death throes unavoidable, at best they could only be prolonged. I just hoped it would not be that night. You see, I loved, I loved being alive.

Enter CIBO *and* VITELLI.

Cibo Your Highness, don't leave the palace.

Duke I have an appointment Cardinal.

Cibo Lorenzo has ordered post-horses, he intends to leave Florence tonight.

Duke I know what Lorenzo is doing tonight.

Vitelli On my way here, your Highness, I happened to notice Lorenzo by the Ponte Trinita. He was jumping about like a mad man.

Duke Perhaps he was drunk, Captain Vitelli.

Vitelli No, when he saw me, he stopped, he just stood and stared. I'm not easily frightened my lord, but that man had the face of a wild animal.

Duke Join me in a glass of wine gentlemen.

Cibo Please listen, my lord.

Vitelli Last night, in the Via Larga, Lorenzo told a number of people, in public, that he was going to kill you.

Duke Were you there Captain?

Vitelli I took the liberty of having him followed.

Duke If you were going to kill me Vitelli, would you be out in the street shouting about it?

Cibo What can we say that will make you believe us?

Duke I do believe you. Have some wine. (DUKE *distributes wine.*) What you don't understand gentlemen is that Lorenzo and I are playing a game.

Cibo Don't go.

Enter LORENZO.

Duke Is it time?

Lorenzo Twelve o'clock. Good evening Vitelli. I saw a travelling player this
evening doing a grotesque impersonation of you.

Vitelli Where?

Lorenzo By the Ponte Trinita. I frightened him off. (*to* DUKE) Hurry my lord,
the lady's waiting.

Duke Which gloves shall I wear Lorenzo? Those of a soldier, or those of a
lover?

Lorenzo Without question, my lord, those of a lover.

Cibo Be careful, your Highness.

Lorenzo Your cloak my lord, it's cold.

LORENZO *puts cloak on* DUKE.

Duke Good night gentlemen.

Lorenzo Good night gentlemen.

They go.

Vitelli We did our best.

Cibo It's the will of God. Prepare for tomorrow.

SCENE 20

An attic. TEBALDEO *is in bed with a* GIRL. PIERO *lies on the floor. Candlelight.*

Piero Are you asleep?

Tebaldeo What's the matter?

Piero I don't know. Frightened, I suppose.

TEBALDEO *gets up.*

Tebaldeo You don't have to go.

Piero It'll be all right.

Tebaldeo I wish I could come with you.

Piero Come on. You've done enough.

Pause.

Tebaldeo You know what I used to say? I'm an artist. And the way I change
the world is through art. Oh, I never went so far as to think it was of any
significance. Just one individual. A grain of sand. A drop in the ocean.
But I thought it was something. A small contribution to the cause of
progress.

Piero You do what you can.

Tebaldeo No, it was all a lie. An excuse.

Piero Most people do nothing.

Tebaldeo Yes. Well, look at me now, working at the Duke's court. I don't
know. I envy you.

Piero I envy you Tebaldeo. You've got a beautiful woman. Between you there's a kind of warmth and softness that I've never known. And perhaps never will.

Tebaldeo It's not because of her. Perhaps I just don't care enough.

Girl Come back to bed.

Tebaldeo I don't even think I'm a coward. I just don't care enough. I wish I did, but I don't.

Piero You gave me shelter.

Tebaldeo I probably did that for myself, to ease my conscience.

The GIRL *gets up. She wraps a blanket around* TEBALDEO.

Girl You'll catch cold.

Tebaldeo What are you afraid of?

Piero Oh, I don't know. Spies. Informers. You can never be sure, and it doesn't help worrying about it either.

Tebaldeo Well, a university is not exactly a closed society. It can't be all that difficult to infiltrate.

Piero No. It's ridiculous.

Tebaldeo Don't go.

Piero It's only a meeting. We haven't made any decisions.

The GIRL *cuddles* TEBALDEO.

Tebaldeo Stay here.

Piero Let's get some sleep, eh?

The GIRL *goes back to bed.* PIERO *lies down on the floor.*

SONG

Tebaldeo (*sings*)
>I'm tired,
>What does he want?
>Why did we come here?
>It's too late.
>Why can't I sleep?
>There's nothing I could do
>What am I now?
>I'm only what I have done
>And what I haven't done.

SCENE 21

LORENZO's *room.* LAUDOMIA *and the* DUKE *together.*

Laudomia (*to the audience*) I loved my country, I loved my brother. I cared about them both. And if I had done nothing, as most people do nothing, I could not have lived with myself.

How self-assured I was, so self-possessed, always in command and in control. I had trained myself to stand outside, denied my sex, denied my life in order to achieve my purpose. Nothing touched me.

But in the end, how strange, events betrayed me. Confused, unsure, everything I'd learned, all those words they sounded foreign to me then. And I who was immune found myself inadequate.

Duke I don't know what to say to you. Funny, isn't it? I've been in this situation with hundreds of other women and I've never been lost for words. I could tell you how beautiful you look. But you've been told that before. I could tell you how I feel about you. But you wouldn't believe me. I could make a joke, if I wasn't so nervous.

Laudomia You are the Duke of Florence, you can do whatever you want.

Duke Talk to me. Tell me about yourself.

Laudomia Let's talk about you.

Duke If only women understand the pressures on men. We are supposed to be the hunters. The conquerors. Whether we want it or not. Sometimes, just once, it would be nice to be hunted.

Laudomia Why do you say that? You're very successful. No-one ever rejects you.

Duke No. Because I've got money, power. Or perhaps it's because I happen to be quite good at stringing together the right words making the right gestures. It's just a game. And I'm tired of that game. I would love to say to someone, quite simply, 'I like you', 'I want you', and for them to say it back to me.

Laudomia What else do you want?

Duke Very little.

Laudomia Shall I tell you what I want?

Duke Yes.

Laudomia For myself, nothing. But for you I would like everything. You're not at all how I imagined you.

Duke Is that a compliment?

Laudomia I'm afraid so.

Duke I don't know whether to say 'thank you'.

Laudomia Do you care what people think of you?

Duke I care what you think.

Laudomia Well, most people have no respect for you at all. They detest you. They're shocked by your behaviour. They despise your government. They're heartbroken by what you've done to their country.

Duke Why don't they say so?

Laudomia They're frightened. My lord, you could win the love of your people. You could gain their respect. You have the opportunity to liberate your country.

Duke Have I?

Laudomia You are young, my lord. You've been badly advised. What could the Pope do if you challenged his authority? The Emperor is too far away, he's in Castille. You've got the garrison on your side, no-one can stop you.

Duke Go on, your ideas interest me.

Laudomia Declare Florence independent. Return power to the Senate. My lord, if you made certain reforms you would win the gratitude of your people. No reward would be too great for you.

Duke I'll do it.

Laudomia You will?

Duke For a woman like you.

Laudomia When?

Duke If wanting to was enough. I'd change immediately. It won't be easy. I'll need your help.

Laudomia I'll be your strength.

Duke Come to bed with me.

Laudomia Now?

Duke I love you.

Laudomia Please. Don't rush me.

Duke How long do you want?

Laudomia How do I know you're telling the truth? Do you really mean to change?

Duke Trust me.

Laudomia Help me. Give me some proof.

Duke But, how do I know I can believe you?

Laudomia Trust me.

Duke (*laughs*) Why should I?

Laudomia For your own sake. You know that your life is in danger.

Duke I know that better than you do.

Laudomia Aren't you afraid?

Duke Take your dress off.

Laudomia No.

Duke I'll tear it off.

Laudomia No.

Duke Come here.

Laudomia No!

Enter LORENZO.

Duke Lorenzo, it's going to be you.

LORENZO *stabs the* DUKE. *Enter* SCORONCONCOLO. *They kill the* DUKE *as* LAUDOMIA *sings.*

LAUDOMIA'S SONG

Laudomia (*sings*)
> I saw a screech-owl in the trees this evening
> In the moonlight as I walked across the garden.
> There was a flower on its own beneath the bushes
> And its petals were the colour of his blood.
>> This room is so cold.
>> What can I do?
>> I'm on my own: I'm just a woman.
>> On my own I can do nothing.

The DUKE *is dead,* LORENZO *has stabbed him six times.* SCORONCONCOLO *has slit his throat.*

Lorenzo (*to the* DUKE) Oh my friend, thank you.
Scoronconcolo My God. It's the Duke of Florence.
Lorenzo You've been paid for what you've done. Now be quiet. This moment is my reward.
Scoronconcolo Oh God.
Laudomia Do you have a pass to leave this city?
Scoronconcolo No. I don't know.
Laudomia Take this ring.

She takes off the DUKE's *ring, gives it to* LORENZO.

Laudomia You've got horses?
Scoronconcolo I don't know. Let's get out of here.
Laudomia You can sell these.

She gives SCORONCONCOLO *some of the* DUKE's *jewellery.*

Scoronconcolo Come on. For God's sake. Come on!
Lorenzo I am Brutus.
Scoronconcolo Oh, Christ!!!

SCORONCONCOLO *runs out.*

Laudomia (*to* LORENZO) Your hand.
Lorenzo He bit my finger. I can see the bone.
Laudomia What are you going to do?
Lorenzo Don't know.
Laudomia Stay in the city.
Lorenzo No.

LAUDOMIA *runs to the door. Rushes back with the key.*

Laudomia There's the key. Lock the door.

LAUDOMIA *runs off.*

Lorenzo (*to* ALESSANDRO) This is our most perfect night. Good-bye my friend. My dear friend. Your life is over, and so is mine.

LORENZO *goes.*

SCENE 22

The DUKE's *Palace.* CARDINAL CIBO *is writing a letter.* CAPTAIN VITELLI *paces up and down.*

Vitelli Declare a state of emergency. Impose a curfew.
Cibo No.
Vitelli There'll be a riot, people in the streets, anarchy!
Cibo I don't think so.
Vitelli The situation demands a show of strength.
Cibo Captain Vitelli, I have assumed power. If you challenge my authority I'll leave for Rome immediately.

Enter 1ST CARDINAL.

1st Cardinal Your Eminence, there's a crowd gathering outside.
Cibo Distribute bread and wine. Declare a public holiday.
1st Cardinal Yes, your Eminence.

Exit 1ST CARDINAL.

Vitelli I hope you know what you're doing.

Enter 2ND CARDINAL.

2nd Cardinal Captain Vitelli.

2ND CARDINAL *hands letter to* VITELLI.

Cardinal Cibo.

2ND CARDINAL *hands letter to* CIBO.

Cibo Thank you.

Exit 2ND CARDINAL.

Vitelli (*reads*) Giacomo de' Medici arrives tomorrow. With his army.
Cibo (*reads*) Lorenzo stopped at Scalperia. He saw a physician.

Enter 3RD CARDINAL.

3rd Cardinal Your Eminence.
Cibo Have you done what I told you?
3rd Cardinal We have placed a guard on Lorenzo's room.
Cibo What happened to the body?
3rd Cardinal We took it to San Lorenzo. Wrapped in a carpet.
Cibo Take this letter. (*to* VITELLI) Captain Vitelli, I need your signature.

Vitelli Right!

VITELLI signs.

Cibo The next Duke of Florence will be Cosimo de' Medici.
Vitelli Who?
Cibo Precisely. He's young, just seventeen, and in the public mind he's not associated with Alessandro.
Vitelli Is that where he lives? Trebbio? That's half a day there, half a day back. Can't we find anyone nearer?
Cibo Who? (*to* 3RD CARDINAL) There's an escort waiting for you. Take this letter to Cosimo. Return with him immediately.

Exit 3RD CARDINAL.

Vitelli And in the meantime, what do we do? Wait for the explosion?
Cibo Whatever happens, we must not provoke it.
Vitelli I am quite capable of being discreet, Cardinal.

Enter 2ND CARDINAL.

2nd Cardinal Francesco Vettori is outside. He wants to talk to you.
Vitelli Arrest him!

VITELLI draws his sword.

Cibo Invite Signor Vettori to come in.
2nd Cardinal Yes, your Eminence.

Exit 2ND CARDINAL.

Cibo Put away your sword Captain Vitelli.
Vitelli (*muttering*) He's a republican.
Cibo I know.
Vitelli (*muttering*) He's got three sons. Conspirators. Saboteurs.
Cibo Captain, would you supervise the distribution of wine?
Vitelli I beg your pardon?
Cibo Get your men to take bread and wine out to the people.
Vitelli My soldiers?
Cibo It's a public holiday. We need a festival atmosphere.
Vitelli A tactic?
Cibo Yes.
Vitelli Right!

VITELLI starts to go. Enter VETTORI.

Vettori In the name of the Republic of Florence, I demand that you surrender power to the Senate.
Cibo Keep the wine flowing Captain Vitelli.

Exit VITELLI.

Vettori Cardinal Cibo, your actions may buy you a little time. They won't save you. The people know that something is wrong.

Cibo Rumours.

Vettori Yes, there are rumours. But I have reason to believe that Alessandro's dead.

Cibo Your belief is correct. He was assassinated by Lorenzo.

Vettori For your own safety Cardinal, dissolve your administration.

Cibo For my safety? On whose behalf are you speaking?

Vettori The citizens of Florence.

Cibo All of them? It always seemed to me that you people weakened your cause with family feuds, doctrinal disputes and a basic lack of loyalty to one another. Signor Vettori, you represent nobody. You merely personify the principle of divide and rule.

Vettori There are hundreds of people outside the palace. They won't be pacified by a few barrels of wine.

Cibo No, they'll get drunk. I can guarantee that. And what have you got to offer them? Your republic has no relevance to the rabble outside. They threaten you as much as they threaten me and I, at least, have the garrison on my side.

Vettori You're prepared to use force?

Cibo If necessary.

Vettori Against unarmed citizens?

Cibo In the last resort, yes.

Vettori I see.

Cibo It is my intention to avoid bloodshed. Signor Vettori, you are a patriot. You are also an intelligent civilised man. Now, how can we as civilised men resolve this terrible crisis?

Vettori You're asking me to help you?

Cibo I'm offering you my protection.

Vettori And if I refuse?

Cibo I'll have you arrested for treason.

Vettori What do you intend to do?

Cibo Tomorrow, Cosimo de' Medici will arrive in Florence. He will be proclaimed Duke.

Vettori What constitutional right have you to impose another Duke?

Cibo I am acting on behalf of the Emperor, and in the interest of all men who desire peace.

Vettori No. I can't accept your proposal.

Cibo Cosimo is not a proposal. The proposal is that we prevent a massacre.

Vettori The people have suffered enough!

Cibo Cosimo will never have the power that Alessandro had.

Vettori How can you guarantee that?

Cibo Alessandro was an embarrassment to us.

Vettori Will you allow the exiles to return?

Cibo You can't guarantee to control them.

Vettori You're offering me nothing.

Cibo If there is no revolution, there will be no arrests. The choice is yours Signor Vettori . . . which is the most important, your principles or human life?

Vettori What do you want me to do?

Enter VITELLI. *He watches.*

Cibo Tell the people that Alessandro is dead. Tell them you support the government. Speak to them. It's an opportunity to save lives.

Vettori Cardinal Cibo, I don't know if you still believe in God, but if you do, I hope he forgives you.

Exit VETTORI *to balcony.*

Vitelli Can you trust him?

Cibo Signor Vettori is a sane, educated gentleman. Return to the citadel. Turn the guns to face the city.

Music. Exit VITELLI. *During* VETTORI's *speech there are moments of song.*

SONG

Vettori My friends, please listen to me. A tragedy has happened. Alessandro is dead. Assassinated by his friend, Lorenzo. Terrible though this event is, we are presented with an opportunity at last, to rectify the errors of the past. Let me be the first, therefore, to welcome the return of law. I am assured the assassin will be outlawed. He will be caught, and made to pay for his crime.

And in this new spirit of legality, we can begin to restore our public life, to rebuild our economy, and rediscover confidence in ourselves and our abilities.

In the end, we are all Florentines. We are united in a common cause. Which will not be served by factions, dissension or conspiracy. No, in the end our success depends on our ability to work together. We are impressed by your demonstration. And as a gesture of good faith, we have proclaimed this day a public day of rest.

Now, please go home, and spend this day among your families. Go home in peace and think upon our tragedy. Our future depends on you and your maturity – to transform tragedy into a national day of hope! Go home.

SCENE 23

The Bargello. PIERO *alone.*

Piero (*to the audience*) We assembled at Prato. Four hundred of us. Florentine students from universities as far apart as Bologna, Pisa, Padua. Our plan was to distribute leaflets in Florence, calling upon the republicans to unite with the exile forces. But events moved so fast, they challenged our imagination. With Alessandro dead, Vitelli's troops on the alert, it became impossible to approach the city. We decided instead to go to Borgo San Sepulcoro, with no less an objective than to capture the fortress and establish a foothold on Florentine territory. We believed that if we could hold the fortress we could inspire a nation to revolt.

We left Prato, marched to Bibbiena, from Bibbiena we marched to Arezzo. We were alive. We believed we were doing something and our lives at last made sense. We looked up at the sky, we saw in the clouds the very images of Plutarch and Demosthenes smiling down upon us. Every town, every village, people watched in silence, and for the moment the whole country held its breath. No sleep. We needed food. Peasants, patricians, priests, every door was slammed in our face, and every refusal inspired us to greater and greater impossibilities.

On the third day we reached Borgo San Sepulcoro. The town was divided between republicans and Medici factions. The fortress was deserted, no resistance, we walked straight in to paradise! Banners. Flags. Flames against a pitch black sky, we danced, we sang, we fell in love that night! Then dawn. A soldier. And a spot of rain.

Enter a SOLDIER.

In the morning we woke to find ourselves surrounded by Vitelli's troops.

More SOLDIERS *enter.*

It rained. For six days and six nights the heavens opened. The wind cut into our bodies, we were hungry, tired, soaked. Arguments broke out, disputes, dissension and finally desertion. There was no attack. Just rain. And on the seventh day, we surrendered.

Under military escort we returned to Florence. A column of rags and tears. We passed familiar landmarks and people left the fields to look at us and laugh. And no doubt that laughter echoes down the centuries.

We entered Florence to unanimous derision. Romantic, immature, poorly planned, badly executed. But at least we did something, we were the only ones who did.

The SOLDIERS *prepare their guns.*

And I still believed that change was inevitable, but I'd learned that change would only be possible when people wanted it, and when their rulers could no longer prevent it.

The SOLDIERS *take aim.*

What would have happened if Alessandro had lived? Would it have made any difference if the assassination had taken place just two days later? Our leaflets might have had a positive effect. The people might at least have been given a chance. I don't know. Perhaps we needed drama to inspire us. I don't know.

VITELLI *gives the signal.* PIERO *is shot.*

SCENE 24

Venice. The balcony of FILIPPO STROZZI's *home.* FILIPPO *alone.*

Filippo (*to the audience*) In many ways I was happier then than I had ever been. I ate well, I drank well, I lived in a house of quite exceptional beauty. All my life I had been a rich man and yet I had never really appreciated money. If it was a nice day I would come out on to the balcony. I had a table there and a chair. I could write letters, entertain friends, I knew a number of people in Venice. Business acquaintances. (*pause*) Sometimes I sat alone for hours. (*pause*) I was an old man, and that was how old men lived. There was time to paint, read, think. And if I couldn't sleep I could always go for a walk. Rich beyond the dreams of more ambitious men. Active in body and mind when younger men were dying or were dead. I had no right to feel dissatisfied when fortune smiled so cruelly on my life.

Enter LORENZO.

Filippo Lorenzo!
Lorenzo This ring once belonged to Alessandro de' Medici.
Filippo What's happened?
Lorenzo This key unlocks the door where his corpse is rotting. Filippo, your daughter is avenged.

FILIPPO *hugs* LORENZO.

Filippo Brutus! You've liberated your country!
Lorenzo Careful. I broke my back getting here.

FILIPPO *releases him.*

Filippo I'm sorry. (*pause*) Alessandro is dead?
Lorenzo And no-one liberated anything.
Filippo There must have been some reaction. People came out into the street? They took up arms?
Lorenzo I'm very tired Filippo.
Filippo What about our friends? Did you warn them?
Lorenzo Oh yes.
Filippo Well.
Lorenzo They finished their suppers, they returned to their games, they went back to sleep.
Filippo Did you tell Corsini?
Lorenzo Everyone.

Filippo And no-one did anything?

Lorenzo What did you expect?

Filippo For six years they've lived with tyranny! – What about Vettori?

Lorenzo At this moment Signor Vettori is probably fencing in his ante-chamber, or drinking with his sons.

Filippo How can you say that?

Lorenzo I didn't wait to find out.

Filippo Why not Lorenzo?

Lorenzo I killed the tyrant, the rest is up to them!

Filippo Yes, anything is possible now. Not every man is capable of doing what you have done, but all men are capable of responding to it. I can't believe that nothing will happen. Do you deny the history of the whole world?

Lorenzo I don't deny history, I just was not there at the time.

Filippo Allow me to call you Brutus. If I'm a dreamer, then allow me that dream. You have made it possible for me to love my country again. Liberty is in the air!

Lorenzo Look over the balcony Filippo. Is there a man down there?

Filippo Where?

They look.

Lorenzo He's been following me all morning.

Filippo What does he want?

LORENZO *takes out a pamphlet.*

Lorenzo (*reading*) 'To any man, noble or commoner, who will kill Lorenzo de Pier Francesco de' Medici, a traitor to his country the Senate of Florence promises the following reward: four thousand gold florins. . . .'

Filippo Where did you get that?

Lorenzo Everywhere.

Filippo You must hide. You must leave Venice.

Lorenzo And then what? The price on my head would follow me.

LORENZO *moves to the balcony.*

Filippo Come away from the balcony.

Lorenzo I came to say good-bye.

Filippo Lorenzo. I can protect you. I've got money. I've got influence.

Lorenzo How could I live with the person I have become? I was a degenerate, I became a murderer, I am now an outlaw.

Filippo Today, but if the wheel turns, tomorrow you could be a saint.

Lorenzo No. I have resolved all my contradictions, except one. I killed Alessandro, that was my reason to live and yet I am not quite ready to face my death.

Filippo Wait, that's all I'm asking you to do.

Lorenzo (*looking out of the window*) The reward is so great, it almost makes him courageous. I wonder if he has a family. Perhaps his children are hungry. He's trying not to look at me. He has my deepest sympathy.

Filippo Stay here. At least for a few days. Who knows what is happening in Florence?

Lorenzo Filippo I have won our bet. The people will not disappoint me. But tell me, do they enjoy oppression? Do they deprive a certain satisfaction from complaining about it? Is their lethargy the expression of some strange happiness? Have they no interest in their own destiny? Is the responsibility, too much for them? And above all, Filippo, are they scared of change?

There is a knock at the door. Silence.

Lorenzo Enter.

A MESSENGER *enters.*

Filippo Who are you?

Messenger My lord, I am employed in the service of Signor Francesco Vettori. He has asked me to tell you that the next Duke of Florence will be Cosimo de' Medici.

The messenger gives FILIPPO *a letter.*

Filippo (*reads*) 'We were frightened of the rabble, they are your enemies as well as ours, we were scared. . . .'

Spotlight on VETTORI.

Vettori (*continues*)' . . . that they might seize what weapons they could and run through the streets robbing and slaying. We saw no swifter remedy than that of electing as head of the city, Cosimo de' Medici. He is a mere youth, but he shows such promise as to offer us reason for hope.

You will say, I see there was no word of me or of my plight, but you must reflect that the fortress we have here above us is an imperial fortress. The fortress at Livorna is held by a Pisan, and another foreigner holds that at Pisa, they are both devotedly imperial. At Levici, there are two thousand five hundred Spaniards. At Genoa, four thousand Germans, and if the imperial agents so much as suspected our intention to swerve from the rule of the Emperor, then these forces would immediately move against us.

My dear Filippo, we have bowed to political reality, and if that does not meet with your approval, please forgive us. Filippo Mio, for the love of God have pity on this poor city, have pity on your friends and kinsmen.'

Spotlight on VETTORI.

Filippo (*continues*) '. . . Elected unanimously by the Senate.' (*to the* MESSENGER) Did nobody speak out against him?

Silence.

Filippo Tell me. Give me one grain of comfort.
Messenger I have no news that will please you.
Filippo Say it.
Messenger At Borgo San Sepulcoro, one hundred students were massacred.
Filippo My son.
Messenger I don't know. I'm sorry.

The MESSENGER *goes.*

Filippo Stay with me Lorenzo.
Lorenzo No. Fresh air. I feel like taking a walk. Good-bye my friend.

Exit LORENZO.

Filippo Good-bye.

FILIPPO *takes pen and paper.*

Filippo (*writing*) I, Filippo Strozzi, having due respect for my soul, commend myself to God and his great mercy . . .

Lights fade.

SCENE 25

A street. Morning. Enter the MERCHANT *and the* GOLDSMITH.

Merchant You look terrible.
Goldsmith I feel great.
Merchant What's the matter with you?
Goldsmith I've done it, my friend, I've finally done it.
Merchant Done what?
Goldsmith Guess.
Merchant Give up.
Goldsmith Look. Today is Coronation day, right?
Merchant Yes.
Goldsmith And I'm a goldsmith, right?
Merchant Yes.
Goldsmith Well?
Merchant Yes?
Goldsmith Look. I've melted down all my gold, took on extra men, haven't slept for three nights. Why?
Merchant Why?
Goldsmith Cosimo coins! That's why! Two thousand little medallions. All in three coloured gold. All with Cosimo's head on them.
Merchant Where are they?
Goldsmith Patience. My man will be here in a minute. I can see it already.

Gondolas up the canal. Nights out at the opera. Venice, my friend. Perhaps you'd visit us sometime? Bring the wife.

Merchant How much did all this cost you?

Goldsmith Everything. I borrowed money. I can't lose. I'll be the only person selling 'em on coronation day, no competition, I can charge what I like. That is free enterprise my friend, the law of supply and demand, get in quick!

Enter a MAN.

Man Excuse me sir.

Goldsmith Where are the coins?

Man They wouldn't give them to me.

Goldsmith Who?

Man The apprentices. The workers. They told me to clear off.

Goldsmith I don't think I'm hearing you very well. What you're saying seems to be coming out funny.

Man They've locked themselves in. They're not coming out till they get paid.

Goldsmith My coins. Get me my coins.

Man That's another thing, they said they're not your coins.

Goldsmith No?

Man They said they made them, they're keeping them.

Goldsmith I must be mad. I've employed a gang of bandits.

Merchant Why don't you give 'em their wages?

Goldsmith I haven't got any money.

Merchant Go to the bank.

Goldsmith The banks are closed. There's a coronation going on!

Merchant They're open tomorrow.

Goldsmith Too late. Everyone'll have Cosimo coins tomorrow. I won't be able to give 'em away. I'm finished. I'm done for. I'm a pauper. Lend me the money.

Merchant If I had it, I would.

Goldsmith I'm your friend!

Merchant I haven't got it!

Goldsmith They're holding me to ransom!

Merchant Sorry.

The GOLDSMITH *starts to go.*

Merchant Look. When I say I haven't got it. I could get it. But it means going to a lot of trouble.

Goldsmith Keep talking.

Merchant Well, for a start, it's going to cost you.

Goldsmith Keep talking.

Merchant Sshh!

MUSIC.

SCENE 26

MUSIC. *The* COMPANY *enter as if at a coronation.*

Cibo My lord, Cosimo de' Medici, you are now Duke of Florence.

Enter COSIMO.

SONG

Cosimo (*sings*)
      Most noble, most powerful lords,
      In return for the favours you have shown
      I offer myself to you.
      I promise, young as I am
      To keep before my eyes for ever
      The fear of God.
      And with the Lord's good grace
      I shall seek to govern in wisdom
      With justice to govern the poor
      And the people with equity,
      So that this city may stand in the judgement
      Blest in the glory of God.

Cibo (*speaks*)
      Now let us call the roll of famous men,
         that were our fathers long ago.
      What high achievements the Lord made known in them
         ever since time began.
      They ruled over kingdoms, issuing to the people
         the commands their times needed.
      Rich they were, furnished with ability, noble
         of aim, and peacefully they dwelt within their homes.

SONG

All (*sing*) These were the glories of our race
      These were the ornaments of our time
      Their sons have left a memorial
      That adds to the glory of their name.

      Not like those others who are forgotten
      In death, as if they had never been

      No, these were men of tender heart
      Their deeds of charity are not forgot
      Blessings on their posterity
      A race set apart for God

Enter LORENZO.

For their sakes this line of theirs
Endures for all time
Their name will never, will never die out.

Enter the MAN.

What though their bodies lie in peace
Their glory lives for evermore
Wherever men assemble
There will their story be told.
Wherever men assemble
There will their story be told.

Everyone leaves except LORENZO *and the* MAN.

EPILOGUE

LORENZO *faces the* MAN *as in the* PROLOGUE.

Man I haven't changed my mind.
Lorenzo Your act will be as futile as mine.
Man My family needs to eat.
Lorenzo Aren't you afraid of what history will say about you?
Man History does not concern me. Yet.
Lorenzo Shall we go somewhere quiet?
Man (*looking around the auditorium*) No. This is perfect.

                                        END OF PLAY